THE GOLDEN AGE OF ROCK

THE GOLDEN AGE OF ROCK

DAVID McCARTHY

CHARTWELL BOOKS, INC.

A QUINTET BOOK

Published by Chartwell Books
A Division of Book Sales, Inc.
110 Enterprise Avenue
Secaucus, New Jersey 07094

ISBN 1-55521-555-9

This book was designed and produced by
Quintet Publishing Limited
6 Blundell Street
London N7 9BH

Creative Director: Peter Bridgewater
Art Director: Ian Hunt
Designer: James Lawrence
Artwork: Danny McBride
Project Editor: Henrietta Wilkinson
Editor: Roger St Pierre
Picture Researcher: Norman Jopling

Typeset in Great Britain by
Central Southern Typesetters, Eastbourne
Manufactured in Hong Kong by
Regent Publishing Services Limited
Printed in Hong Kong by
Leefung-Asco Printers Limited.

CONTENTS

THE BEATLES

INTRODUCTION

Any voyage through the vastly over-charted yet still murky waters of rock and pop history is faced with one major problem. Not so much who should go in, but rather who should be left out. Is Little Richard more important than Chuck Berry? Should the maverick genius of country music's Johnny Cash have a place in the tale? Is the story of Stax any less important than that of Motown?

One person's beat is another's noise pollution, and so any mixture of ingredients is bound to offend someone's own pop sensibility. Within the framework of the following words is an attempt to mark out a linear progression of rock and pop music. Most of the records that provide the soundtrack for the contents are still widely available and stand the test of time. The aim of this book is to tell the story, in words and pictures, of the characters and events that came together to produce the Golden Age of Rock.

Thanks are due to both Judith and Mike, without whom . . . and also to Caron for use of her office.

This book is for Peter and his love of Elvis.

OPPOSITE PAGE
Clockwise from top: The Rolling Stones in Hyde Park, 1969; James Dean in classic rebel icon pose; UK 1950s bad boy Cliff Richard; The Beatles as cardboard cut-outs.

BELOW
GI Elvis signs name, rank and number.

THE BLUES HAD A BABY AND THEY CALLED IT ROCK AND ROLL

1

New Year's Eve 1949 saw the Western world emerging from the most turbulent decade of its history. Most of the developed nations, counting the massive cost of worldwide conflict, were trying to restart and reshape their industries and economies.

The United States was one of the first to return to peace-time production. Having been spared the ruinous saturation bombing suffered by much of Europe, industry in the US was well placed to turn its hand away from armaments and towards the technological revolution of leisure and labour-saving devices.

The basic foundations had already been laid and tested. The Henry Ford vision of the all-important production lines led to whole towns being dominated by a product in much the same way that communities had grown up around mining concerns in the past. From the extraction and processing of raw materials, through assembly and testing, a city such as Detroit, which became known as 'Motor City', stands as a perfect example of a large area dedicated to auto production.

ABOVE, RIGHT
Glen Miller in the 1930s.

OPPOSITE
American families became the world's first consumer class in the 1950s.

Cars, televisions, refrigerators, radios and domestic appliances started rolling off production lines in numbers previously unthought of. On their brand-new TV sets, American families saw advertisements for a torrent of luxury hardware. Revitalized industries provided much-needed employment, causing over one million black Americans to move to the northern factory-based cities and with them a migration of musical cultures. The new-found prosperity was soon to give the teenaged 'war babies' double the spending power that their parents had enjoyed at a similar age.

At the time, many varied musical strands were running through American culture. The charts, such as they were, almost exclusively contained crooning men and romantically inclined, wholesome, girls. Doris Day and Rosemary Clooney partnered Fred Astaire, Bing Crosby and Eddie Fisher as stereotypes of the relaxed, easy-going genre.

Solo singers were a recent phenomenon. Up until the mid-1940s, the main function of a singer was as a featured vocalist with one of the big bands: Benny Goodman had Peggy Lee, Glen Miller had Ray Eberle. The man who broke the mould was Frank Sinatra.

BELOW
Glen Miller, third from left, with band members, wives and girlfriends.

Sinatra had been the vocalist with the Harry James band before moving on to Tommy Dorsey's outfit. But by 1942, he was established enough to strike out on his own. His easy-going phrasing and relaxed timing recalled the crooners, but his good looks led him to become the first true pop star pin-up, and his live shows frequently saw him besieged by screaming 'bobbysox' fans.

A large part of the music industry was being run by Italian Americans; coupled with Sinatra's success, this resulted in a whole string of singers, including Frankie Laine, Buddy Greco, Perry Como, Tony Bennett and Dean Martin, who played heavily on their romantic style and Mediterranean good looks.

Sinatra himself made many classic recordings, often backed by the quick-silver arrangements of Nelson Riddle, before he moved to Hollywood, stretching his appeal far beyond the screaming teenagers of the 1940s with his sophisticated, elegantly relaxed image.

At the other end of the musical spectrum stood Huddie Ledbetter. Born in 1885, and better known as 'Leadbelly', his teenage years were those of a penniless black American in the Deep South at the turn of the century. Having already escaped from one chain gang, Leadbelly was convicted of murder in 1917 and sentenced to 30 years imprisonment. He languished in penal obscurity until the late 1930s, when he was discovered by the Lomax brothers while on their historic trek around the cotton fields and penitentiaries of the southern states, documenting and preserving the last exponents of the black folk music in the Deep South. With the primitive recording equipment at their disposal they cut tracks with Leadbelly singing in his gruff voice and playing guitar in a distinctive, brutal, style. These recordings, which were cut straight on to disc, are the source of songs like *House of the Rising Sun, Midnight Special, John Handy* and *Goodnight Irene.*

OPPOSITE

Huddie Ledbetter, or 'Leadbelly', the seminal bluesman whose music influenced several subsequent generations.

Although Leadbelly died before 1949, the cross-cultural seeds that he had sown were to prove vitally important to the complex black music scene as younger men, such as Robert Johnson, carried the blues forward. Johnson was still in his 20s when he died in 1938, but he left behind songs such as *Love in Vain, Dust my Broom* and *Crossroad Blues,* all of which would be plundered almost note-for-note by the young white guitar heroes of the 1960s. Men such as Son House and Tommy Johnson, with their savage slide guitar and world-weary vocals, in turn provided the inspiration for the next generation of bluesmen, based in Chicago.

ABOVE

Muddy Waters, the embodiment of the 'Chicago' sound.

When Muddy Waters cut *I Can't be Satisfied* in 1947, he crystalized the essence of the Chicago sound. With screaming bottleneck slide, a slap bass and

ABOVE
Howlin' Wolf, one of the stars on the Chess label.

his special voice, Waters opened the floodgates for the new wave of talent that was already playing in the bars and streets of Chicago.

Several independent local labels sprang up to cater for the new demand, the strongest of these being Chess and its sister label Checker. Owned by two Polish-Jewish immigrants, Len and Phil Chess, the labels soon dominated the scene. The brothers also ran the Macomba, a well-known club, and WVON, the city's leading black radio station, with the result that the Chess empire largely defined the Chicago sound, although other labels, like Vee Joy with Jimmy Reed also played a part. By the early 1950s Muddy Waters had formed a five-piece band which included second guitarist Jimmy Rogers, pianist Otis Span and Little Walter on harmonica. Together they cut the definitive Chicago sides on the Chess label, with tracks such as *Hoochie Coochie Man* and *Got My Mojo Working.*

Another Chess artist who had his roots in Delta blues but was a leading exponent of the Chicago sound was Howlin' Wolf. After he moved to the city he recorded *Smokestack Lightning* for the label, and went on to supply them with over a decade's worth of classic cuts. BB King too was a product of the Deep South who progressed North and West to find a wider audience for his West Coast sound. After service during the war, King became a DJ on station WDIA in Memphis. It was here that he started performing in clubs and bars, going on to play throughout the South following the release of his seminal

BELOW, LEFT
Charlie 'Bird' Parker, taking it to the limit.

BELOW, RIGHT
A young B.B. King, pictured here without his guitar 'Lucille'.

million-seller *3am Blues,* recorded in Memphis but leased to a West Coast label.

Far removed from the harsh, guttural blues of Chicago, his bands often featured brass instruments, and were led by his own fluent bursts of often jazz-tinged guitar. In fact, BB King and his guitar 'Lucille' were the role models for the 1960s guitar hero superstars Eric Clapton and Jeff Beck, who re-ran King's formula for the vast rock crowds nearly 20 years later, and in doing so turned him into a major international star whose career prospers to this day.

The blues was a large musical family, whose close relatives included gospel, with its joyous messages of salvation and deep-rooted emotional effect, and its secular counterpart, the emergent soul music, which found its form and its name at the tail end of the 1950s through the work of Ray Charles and Sam Cooke. But perhaps the most interesting of all was jazz.

Sailing close to the artistic edge, often fuelled by drugs such as heroin and amphetamines, technical wizards Miles Davis and Charlie Parker were stretching musical boundaries, taking standards and

LEFT
The mercurial talents of Miles Davis mutated jazz into previously unimagined shapes.

twisting their tempos and tonalities almost beyond recognition. But although the end result won a large and devoted following, it was ultimately too eclectic and, some would say, sophisticated for acceptance by the wider mass audience.

But while these, and many other, musical strands existed in America at the start of the 1950s the country was still firmly a white, Anglo-Saxon Protestant (WASP) hegemony, and as such was not open to its own wealth of culture. The image of WASP America was perpetuated by the entertainment industry, with Hollywood as the propaganda machine, where even top-grossing stars were required to anglicize their ethnic immigrant names.

But even the movie-making Hollywood suburb of Los Angeles was to be invaded by the demands of the teenaged war babies. Two films, *The Wild One* and *Rebel Without a Cause,* starring Marlon Brando and James Dean respectively, were to place on celluloid the nascent image of the surly, aggressive teenager searching for an identity. In the *Wild One,* someone asks of Brando: 'What are you rebelling against?', to which he languidly replies, 'What have you got?'

Although featuring music more suited to the traditional Hollywood big band style, both films became rallying points for the disaffected youth of America. With kids getting a driving licence at 15, the mass ownership of cars, and over 3,000 drive-in cinemas by 1952, the strands were being pulled together to create the first true youth culture.

With books like Jack Kerouac's seminal 'beat' novel *On the Road,* starring an anti-hero who openly envied the black lifestyle, and with thousands of those car radios belonging to white kids constantly tuned into the black music stations, the WASP moral majority were about to come face-to-face with a youth movement they could neither appreciate nor understand.

RIGHT
Brando, in *The Wild One,* rebelling against anything you've got.

BELOW
James Dean, the face of a generation searching for an identity.

BIG PINK CARS AND ELECTRIC GUITARS 2

As early as 1951 a shrewd ex-boxer turned publisher named Morris Levy had patented the words 'Rock and Roll'. But only a couple of months later, the US courts overturned the patent on the grounds that the phrase had passed into the public domain.

RIGHT
A young Chuck Berry, the inventor of the pop song as it stands today. On drums: Berry's friend DJ Alan Freed, the man who coined the phrase 'Rock and Roll'.

Although the music was still not widely heard, it was being loudly praised by disciples in high places. One such was Alan Freed, who is generally credited with having coined the phrase in the first place. Freed's career began spinning records on radio station WSW in Cleveland, where his shows featured a strict diet of R&B cuts accompanied by Freed thumping out the backbeat with his fist. But it was his live shows, *The Moondog Rock 'n' Roll Party,* that caused the biggest stir. The events drew what was known as a 'chessboard' crowd – an almost equal mix of black and white alike. This was remarkable for a time

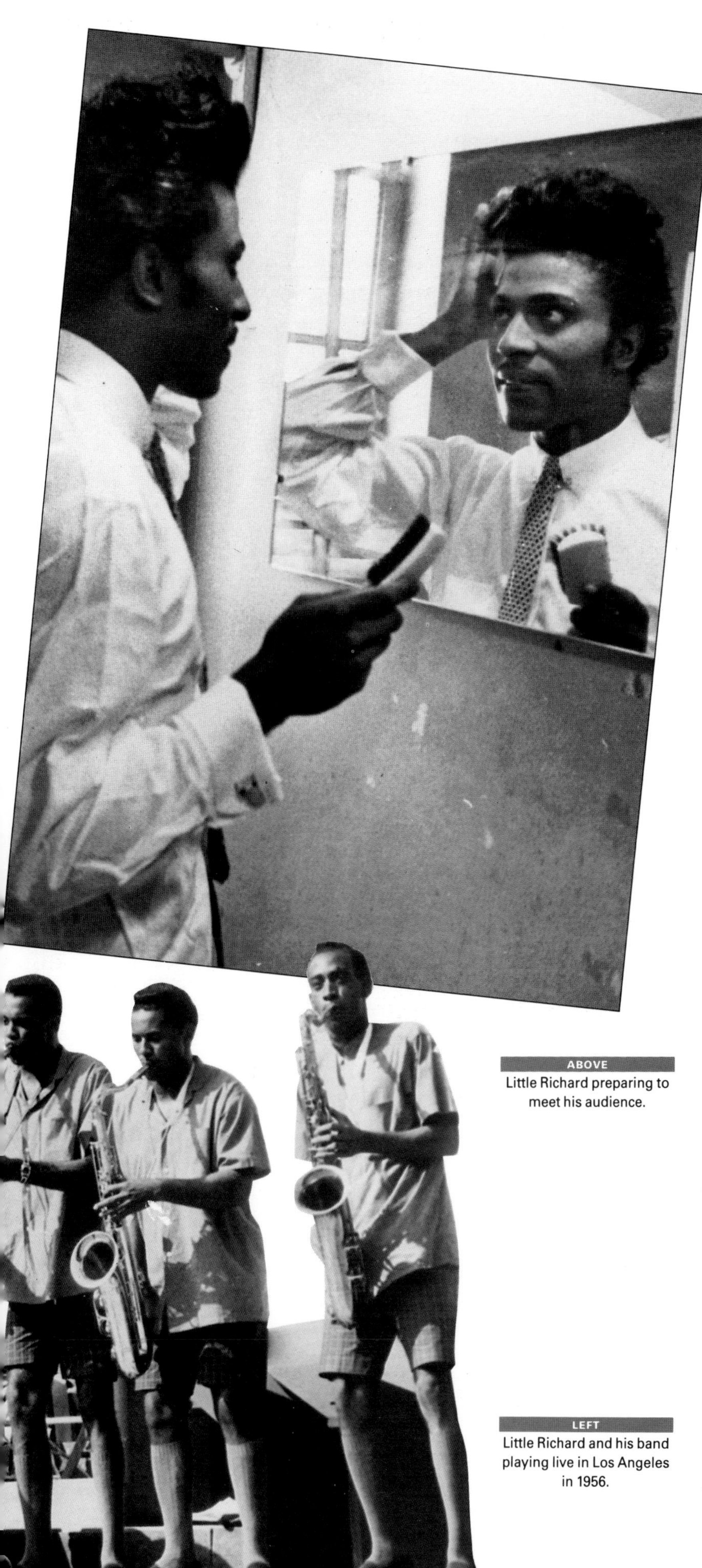

ABOVE
Little Richard preparing to meet his audience.

LEFT
Little Richard and his band playing live in Los Angeles in 1956.

in which far more than the music scene was run on the basis of racial segregation. In fact, Cleveland was a mainly segregated city, and one of Freed's shows was cancelled by police after attracting a total of over 20,000 black and white fans.

After he made the move to New York, where he broadcast with station WINS, Freed continued to promote live shows – mainly booking acts into the Paramount Theater. At one time or another over the next few years, almost all of the major rock 'n' roll, R&B and rockabilly stars played one of his bills. It was at the Paramount in 1956, that Chuck Berry invented his famous 'duckwalk' live onstage, some say as a ruse to hide his ill-fitting trousers.

Berry was in his mid-20s in 1955. He was the first songwriter to talk directly to the postwar youth in the language they used and concerning the things that they cared about. In *Maybelline,* released the same year, Berry tells of an argument with his girlfriend, who, when she drives off in her Coupé de Ville cadillac, is pursued by Berry, in his V8 Ford, in a 100 miles per hour car chase. In *Schooldays* a feeling of tight, stifled classroom boredom, and the subsequent liberating release of jukebox-generated rock and roll sounds, is captured. Other songs, such as *Carol, Little Queenie* and *Sweet Little Sixteen,* all feature Chuck Berry's other main pecadillo: girls. Each song paints a different picture of essentially the same person – high heels, tight dresses, lipstick and curls – usually to be found standing next to the all-important jukebox. But perhaps the best example of Berry's craft is the later *No Particular Place to Go.* In this tune, basically a reworking of *Schooldays,* his twin obsessions of girls and cars are interwoven and laced with suggestive wit. After setting the scene by telling us he's driving round with his 'baby' beside him, having just 'stolen a kiss', Berry sings:

The night was young and the air was bold,
So we decided to take a stroll,
Can you imagine the way I felt?
I couldn't unfasten her safety belt.

Added to these titles like *Around and Around, Roll Over Beethoven, Johnny B. Goode* and *Rock and Roll Music,* are all that is needed to confirm the contribution his body of work made to modern music: it

ABOVE
Sun Records' Sam Phillips with Jerry Lee Lewis.

LEFT
Elvis Aaron Presley, the world's first pop superstar.

could well be argued that Chuck Berry invented the pop song as we know it today.

But Berry was not operating in a vacuum. Richard Penniman, better known as Little Richard, was also plugged into the rock 'n' roll mains' supply. He was only 20-years-old when, with the opening scream of 'Awopbopaloobopalopbamboom' he crashed his song *Tuttifrutti* into the national charts and went on to sell well over two million copies. Richard had a background of church and gospel singing and he unleashed an almost religious fervour into his performances. Dressed in large, loud suits in pink and gold lamé, he would leap on to his piano and beat out melodies with his foot. Crashing to the floor, he would writhe around with his microphone while belting out one rocker after another, most of which were clothed in thinly-veiled innuendo.

Follow-up tracks included impressive hits like *Rip it Up* and *Long Tall Sally,* which are both now rock and roll standards, but a couple of years later Little Richard renounced rock 'n' roll for the calling of God. He became a church minister and sang only gospel music, with a corresponding change in his previously wildly untamed appearance. Later on, he returned to rock 'n' roll and, over the years, his performances became more camp.

At the beginning of the 1950s, Sam Phillips had taken up a job as disc jockey on station WRAC in Memphis, where he had moved after his war service.

Soon realizing that there was a dire lack of facilities to record the Memphis sound found in bars and on the streets, Phillips opened Sun recording studios in 1950. Early customers included Howlin' Wolf, BB King, Rufus Thomas and Bobby Bland, and for the first few years, Phillips sold the sides he cut to the big blues and R&B labels of the day, Chess and Modern. In 1953 he started his own label, Sun Records. It was a local independent concern that ran on a shoestring budget, so to make extra money he also ran a subsidiary, the Memphis Recording Company, looked after by an ex-'Miss Radio of Memphis', Marion Keisker.

One Saturday afternoon a young man took his place in the queue at the studios at 706 Union Avenue, with the intention of paying $4.00 to cut a 10in acetate for his mother's birthday. Accompanied by his battered guitar, Elvis Presley cut two songs – *That's Where Your Heartache Begins,* and *My Happiness,* which had been a hit for a popular black group called the Inkspots. Miss Keisker was so impressed that she managed to record a part of the first and all of the second song on to a spare length of tape which she later

RIGHT
Elvis on stage with long-time cohorts Scotty Moore and Bill Black.

played to her boss Phillips (who did not share her enthusiasm).

At that time, Elvis Aaron Presley lived with his family in Memphis. He earnt about $40.00 a week driving a truck for the Crown Electric Company, and his only ambition was to own the coolest car in town. Born the only survivor of identical twins on January 8, 1935 in a two-room log cabin in Tupelo, Mississippi, his father Vernon struggled hard to provide for his family. This meant a move to Memphis when Elvis was 13-years-old, a shy, polite child who liked nothing more than to tune into the predominantly black blues' radio stations.

Eight months after his first visit to Sun studios, he returned to record another demo, this time cutting two tracks with Sam Phillips in attendance. A week later Phillips had a new song he wanted to demo and he decided to give 'the kid with the sideburns' a try. Presley did not take to the

LEFT
Elvis, Scotty and Bill, then known as 'The Blue Moon Boys' playing in a session in 1954.

BELOW
Elvis pictured with his manager and mentor 'Colonel' Tom Parker, who some would say sanitized Presley's raw appeal too much.

ABOVE
The newly crowned 'King' meets the elder statesman of rock and roll, Bill Haley.

song, and ended up running through a long and varied selection of personal favourites, including the blues, gospel, country and chart hits of the day.

In an effort to harness the boy's talents, Sam Phillips introduced Elvis to a young guitar player called Scotty Moore. Acoustic bass player Bill Black was added last, and the threesome spent some months hammering out their own basic style before Phillips booked the three lads into the studio on Monday 6 July, 1954, to record some tracks. When Presley started to play with an old Arthur 'Big Boy' Crudup song, changing the words and tune, Phillips knew he was witnessing something important. For some time he had jokingly said that a white boy who could sing like a black man would make him a billion dollars, and at that point he badly wanted to get the sound coming from his small studio on to tape.

The outcome of the session was Sun 209; *That's All Right (Mama)* backed with *Blue Moon of Kentucky*. When an acetate of the tracks was played on the 'Red Hot and Blue' show on Radio WHBQ by DJ Dewey Phillips, the station was besieged with calls. Later that evening Elvis was rushed from a cinema to the station's studio for an on-air interview. The sensational response was largely provoked by the fact that listeners could not believe that the voice belting out *That's All Right* belonged to a white man, and Presley convinced the audience by explaining that he had attended Hume High School, a whites-only establishment. The single went on to sell over 20,000 copies, despite a battle against the racially-orientated programming of radio stations at the time.

Elvis and his band played their first live date in July of that year at the Overton Park open-air theatre, before going on to release four more singles on Sun over the next 18 months. But by this time Elvis's live act was causing more than a passing interest. His mere appearance horrified

ABOVE
The once shy Elvis strikes an informal pose whilst chatting to an extra during the filming of *Jailhouse Rock*.

RIGHT
Private Presley, E, US Army 53310761.

most American adults, as his heavily greased hair, long sideburns and a preference for loud pinks and bright colours challenged accepted values, but worse still was his behaviour onstage.

Presley just could not keep still. He said that he had never known a time when music did not move him, quite literally, but it was the way he moved that caused so much apoplexy. With his knee drops, thrusting hips and his arrogant sneer, Elvis prompted the Reverend Carl E. Elgena, the pastor of a Baptist church in Des Moines, to call him 'morally insane'.

This attention did not deter the major labels, however. Ahmet Ertagun was the first to offer and was prepared to hock his independent but nationally distributed Atlantic label to the hilt if his $25,000 carrot were to be taken. But it was RCA Victor that Phillips finally struck a deal with, to the tune of $35,000. For this sum, Phillips not only signed away the rights to Presley but also to all the tracks his star had recorded at Union Avenue, both released sides and otherwise. Presley himself made $5,000 on the deal, and went out and bought a brand new cadillac – pink, of course.

It was at this point that 'Colonel' Tom Parker offered his managerial services to Presley. Parker (the rank was self-appointed but its use insisted upon) was an ex-fairground hustler who always played his cards close to his chest, and Elvis was impressed enough to hire him straight away. Next to join the team was drummer DJ Fontana, and it was as a four-piece that the group undertook a full tour of the southern United States. In February of 1956, they went into the RCA studios in Nashville to record *Heartbreak Hotel*. The track, the first for RCA, stuck closely to the heavily reverbed yet rich and crisp sound that was the trademark of Phillips' Sun studio, making the most of a winning formula, but by now Presley's live appearances were causing even greater comment. After slots on both the Dorsey Brothers and the Jackie Gleason TV shows, outraged reviews centred on Presley's 'too sexy' act, with descriptions of him ranging from 'male burlesque dancer' to the plain 'obscene'.

Although Parker managed to strike a deal for three performances by Elvis on the important coast-to-coast Ed Sullivan

show, Presley was not allowed to hold his guitar, and was shot only from the waist up. Nonetheless, his appearance on the show caused further sensation, and with the extensive resources of RCA behind him, Presley suddenly found his career starting to skyrocket.

Don't Be Cruel, *Hound Dog* and *Love Me Tender* were all massive hits the same year, the latter being the first record ever to go 'gold' on the strength of advance sales alone.

By April '56 Tom Parker had laid out his strategy: why send Elvis out to play live, so risking possible anticlimax, when he could play to millions through the movies? With his hair dyed jet black, Presley's first two films presented him as a kind of singing James Dean, but the third, *Jailhouse Rock*, was a different matter entirely. With Elvis responsible for much of the slick choreography, as well as a scene where he is flogged by a sadistic warder, this feature-movie was undoubtedly Presley's strongest film offering. The title song sequence is perhaps his best celluloid moment.

But although Elvis Presley was the hottest property in the American entertainment industry – and probably the most famous man worldwide in the under 25 age group – he was still faced with the great leveller: the US Army Draft Board, the scourge of young American males. Conscription had been in operation since World War II, and in March 1958 Elvis received his call-up papers. On the 20th of that month he reported to the Memphis Draft Board offices at 6.30 am and became Private Presley, E, US Army 53310761.

Over the next few months there were many publicity shots featuring GI Elvis – the sideburns meeting a barber's blade, the collection of standard-issue kit,

ABOVE:
Right to left: Buddy Holly, Don Everly, Jerry Lee Lewis, and friend Jimmy Velvet.

RIGHT
Presley before meeting the US Army barber's blade.

Presley on parade – as a vast promotional machine was set in motion for the good of the Army, as much as for Elvis' career. RCA continued to release tracks from their stockpile at regular intervals, including some of the unreleased Sun sessions, and in the two years since he had first cut Sun 209, Elvis had more than 20 worldwide million-sellers. Songs like *Blue Suede Shoes* and *All Shook Up* carried on his rockabilly roots, while tracks such as *Teddy Bear* opened up a wider audience. 'I knew Elvis would be big,' Sam Phillips was to say, 'but I never knew he'd be that big.'

Due in large part to the success of Presley, but also influenced by the altruistic beginnings of the studio and his own reputation, many other talented artists beat a path to Phillips' door. Jerry Lee Lewis was one such, arriving uninvited at Sun before talking Phillips into giving him an audition session. Lewis fitted in well with the spirit at Union Avenue, when late night stints would often turn into riotous parties. Jerry Lee's roots were firmly based in a country style, and he himself views classic rockers like *Whole Lotta Shakin'* and *Great Balls of Fire* as country records, but his fiery delivery was definitely coming from rock 'n' roll. His hard reputation for living life to the full made him the centre of controversy, both on stage and off.

FAR LEFT
Jerry Lee Lewis in a not-so-wild publicity pic for *Whole Lotta Sharin' Going On.*

LEFT
Carl Perkins, another Sun studio success, whose songwriting credits include Blue Suede Shoes.

ABOVE
Buddy Holly and the Crickets pictured in 1957, shortly before their first hit 'That'll Be The Day.'

His main trouble came about when the media discovered he had married his third wife five months before his divorce from the second became final. And to add to that his new bride was only 13-years-old and his cousin to boot! This was just a few short months after Chuck Berry had been charged with 'transporting a minor across State lines for immoral purposes', in violation of the Mann Act.

Jerry Lee Lewis was not the only, nor by any means the most famous, name to search out Phillips. Carl Perkins, already a well-known artist in country and rockabilly circles, made use of the distinctive Sun sounds, writing *Blue Suede Shoes*, a big hit for himself as well as for Elvis Presley, in the process. Roy Orbison, the 'Big O', also cut tracks with Phillips, and his Sun single *Ooby Dooby* went on to sell over 350,000 copies.

Many legendary sessions took place in the studio on Union Avenue, but possibly the greatest came one sultry afternoon in August 1956. Sam Phillips gathered together a star-studded four-piece band – Elvis on piano, Carl Perkins and Johnny Cash on guitars, and Jerry Lee Lewis singing. This 'million dollar quartet' recorded two takes of *Peace in the Valley*, neither of which has ever been commercially released.

While Sam Phillips had created his own stylized sound by treating a performance with heavy reverb and an accent on spontaneity, it was Norman Petty, down in Texas, who made a great leap forward for the pop record towards the end of the decade.

Although the first function of a record was essentially to be a solid reminder of a live band or singer, 1950s development of multi-tracking, pioneered by people like Les Paul, meant studio technique was becoming increasingly important, and led the record to develop its own identity. Petty was co-writer and producer for Buddy Holly and the Crickets. He began by creating songs in the studio, giving them arrangements that defined them as studio- not performance-based. Some of Holly's records of the time are perfect pointers to the Beatles' later pop sensibility, but unfortunately, Buddy Holly's career was cut short in the plane crash which also claimed the lives of Richie Valens and the under-rated Big Bopper, whose *Chantilly Lace* was a hit in 1958.

BELOW
Buddy Holly and the Crickets, who together with producer Norman Petty pioneered studio recording techniques.

SOMEWHERE OVER THE OCEAN 3

Great Britain was not a fun place in which to be a teenager in the early 1950s. Unlike the United States, which was about to jump headfirst into a leisure-orientated consumer maelstrom, the 'land fit for heroes' was struggling to rebuild its shattered post war economy. At the time, the live musical circuit in the UK was mainly controlled by the two big chains, Mecca and Top Rank, who between them owned most of the large dance halls in major towns. The sound that emerged from these buildings, known grandly as the Locarno, the Palais or something similar, was an extension of the big band era of the previous decade. Revolving stages brought a different ensemble of jobbing musicians in to play every half-hour, signs declared 'no jiving', and intimidating bouncers in tuxedos produced an end result of highly-regulated, closely controlled, approved entertainment.

BOTTOM OF PAGE
The fake grandeur of the big band dance halls.

BELOW
Jack Jackson, whose Radio Luxembourg show claimed wide influence.

The airwaves in Britain suffered similar strictures. The British Broadcasting Corporation (BBC) controlled the only two radio stations in the country as well as one of the television channels; the other TV network was independently owned, but heavily restricted as to its advertising and content. As a consequence, the first blast

RIGHT
Lock up your daughters, it's Bill Haley and the Comets!

FAR RIGHT
Bill Haley, who brought rock and roll commotion to British cinemas, dance halls and front pages.

of musical excitement to hit Britain in the 1950s arrived through the cinema. *Rock Around the Clock*, a fairly unremarkable film that ran for just over an hour and featured a shallow plot, opened around the country in 1956, causing a considerable commotion. At the centre of the storm stood a fat-faced Bill Haley and his backing group, the Comets.

Born in Detroit in 1927, Haley was already nearly 30-years-old – and married with five children – by the time he was arousing teenage passions. The title song became a huge worldwide hit, written by a couple of Tin Pan Alley hacks, one of whom was 63-years-old! The popular press were quick to pick up on this unprecedented outburst of teenage enthusiasm, demonstrated by the fact that when Haley and his band arrived to tour Britain a year later they were met by more than 2,000 fans at Waterloo train station in London.

The BBC monopoly of the radio airwaves did have one small crack, however. In bedrooms all over the country small radios were being tuned into the faint interference-riddled signals emanating from Radio Luxembourg. The *Jack Jackson Show* and the imported Alan Freed shows were spinning sides from people like Elvis and Little Richard, and the actual activity of tuning into Luxembourg had an almost covert, clandestine connotation; 'out there', others were picking up on the same rock 'n' roll gospel of teenage salvation.

Quite by chance, two other diverse imports came together to provide a fertile breeding-ground for the germination of British pop. The jukebox arrived from the United States and found its home in an

I WANT TO HOLD YOUR HAND The Beatles
GLAD ALL OVER The Dave Clark Five
SHE LOVES YOU The Beatles
YOU WERE MADE FOR ME Freddie & The Dreamers
I ONLY WANT TO BE WITH YOU Dusty Springfield
24 HOURS FROM TULSA Gene Pitney
DOMINIQUE The Singing Nun
SECRET LOVE Kathy Kirby
SWINGIN' ON A STAR Big Dee Irwin
HIPPY HIPPY SHAKE Swinging Blue Jeans
MARIA ELENA Los Indios Tabajaras
DON'T TALK TO HIM Cliff Richard
I WANNA BE YOUR MAN The Rolling Stones
THE BEATLES (L.P.) The Beatles

LEFT
Jimmy Saville, in the jukebox-like set of Top of the Pops in the early 1960s.

idea taken from Italy – the coffee bar.

The Coffee Cup, which opened in Hampstead in the mid-1950s, was one of the first such bars in the country. With an espresso machine that could produce 100 cups of foaming Capuccino from 1 lb (0.4 g) of coffee, it soon became a hit with teenagers looking for a new environment to call their own, away from the outdated dance halls and pubs that their parents frequented. The general opinion of coffee bars was one of imported decadence, a view which was, as usual, fuelled by the press, but it did nothing to halt their rapid proliferation. In fact, by 1958 there were over 3,000 such establishments across the country, one of the best-known of which was the Two I's in London's Soho.

It was in the Two I's that John Kennedy, a young publicity agent, met Tommy Hicks, a junior seaman, with a crooked smile and big ambitions, who was playing guitar and singing covers of recent American hits. Kennedy was no great fan of rock 'n' roll, finding it mildly distasteful and a potentially bad influence on the nation's

BELOW
The Two I's coffee bar in London's Soho, an important meeting place in the late 1950s and early 1960s.

youth, but here he saw an opportunity to clean it up. Anglicizing the raw form for consumption by a domestic market, Kennedy presented Britain's first true home-grown pop star – Tommy Steele.

A press campaign showed Steele playing at upper-class debutantes' balls, with young girls fighting over the chirpy cockney lad, and Kennedy even went so far as to take a photo of the Duke of Kent

ABOVE
Larry Parnes, seen here with one of his more successful creations Marty Wilde.

leaving a West End theatre and give it to the press with a caption implying the Duke had just seen a Tommy Steele performance. Before the year was out, Steele was a regular in the charts and had starred in his own film. Kennedy decided to take on a partner in his management company, a young man called Larry Parnes, whose background was in the retail clothing trade. Kennedy was happy to have just one star but Parnes – 'they don't call me Mr Parnes shillings and pence for nothing' – saw the chance to create a whole stable of artists, reselling the same formula. Steele was followed by a host of outrageously named personalities, including Marty Wilde, Johnny Gentle, Dickie Pride, Vince Eager and Billy Fury.

Fury's story is a classic example of the star maker in action. Born Ronald Wincherly in 1941 in Liverpool, and blessed with the classic arrogant looks of a pin up, the young man was a keen rockabilly fan, and thought himself a good enough songwriter to earn a living from it. On one occasion when a Parnes package, featuring Marty Wilde, was playing in Birkenhead in 1958, Wincherly jumped the ferry and talked his way into the star's dressing room to play his songs. Wilde liked them so much that he called in Parnes, who invited Wincherly to perform

RIGHT AND BELOW
Britain's first true indigenous pop star, Tommy Steele.

LEFT
Billy Fury, né Ronald Wincherly.

as the opening act on that night's bill. So Billy Fury made his live debut, and directly he finished his set, Parnes signed him up.

Fury went on to become a respected star, perhaps the first British rock 'n' roll star, as opposed to Steele's pop version. His rockabilly roots showed through his Carl Perkins' influenced songs, and his onstage displays gave rise to a deal of fan hysteria. His deliberately provocative displays of sexuality quite literally drove crowds into a frenzy, but his recorded output on Decca remains a testament to his real love of music, standing as perhaps the finest home-produced rock 'n' roll of its day.

Many of Parnes' stars had one thing in common – they all took Elvis as the blueprint and watered down his style for British consumption. But the teenager with perhaps the biggest 'King' obsession was not one of the Parnes clique; his name was Harry Webb and he had his Presley impersonation down to a tee. His low-slung guitar, hooked lip sneer, greased back hair and long sideburns were all too much for TV's Jack Good, the producer behind the hit shows *6-5 Special* and *Oh Boy*. Good advised the young singer to tone down his act, and the cleaner cut, sideburn-free Webb became Cliff Richard. Cliff's first hit, *Move It* in 1958, propelled him into the charts and finally on to *Oh Boy*, where home-grown stars such as Marty Wilde mainly sang covers of American hits.

But after this promising start *Move It* was arguably the best of the British rock 'n' roll offerings of the 1950s – Cliff soon succumbed to pressures to adapt his act to

RIGHT
Billy Fury was the closest UK rocker to rival Presley's raw sex appeal.

RIGHT AND BOTTOM RIGHT
Cliff Richard, whose early raunchiness soon gave way to a middle of the road broad-based appeal.

a middle-of-the-road approach. Eventually recognized as an all-round family entertainer, films like *Expresso Bongo* and *The Young Ones*, together with spin-off tracks like *Living Doll*, diluted Cliff's original rebel teenage appeal, and he became another wholesome boy-next-door, aimed at the kids and their parents alike.

On his many tours, Cliff was backed by a group who called themselves the Drifters and who were an assortment of musicians put together for the shows. Around late 1958, the line-up stabilized into that of Bruce Welch and Hank Marvin on guitars, Jet Harris on bass and Tony Meehan on drums. The band won a recording deal in their own right and released several singles, which were much in the style of the Everly Brothers' close harmonies. In fact, Jack Good went so far as to say that Hank and Bruce's vocal duets made the Drifters the best vocal group in the country.

However, Atlantic records in America had a black act also called the Drifters on their books – an act with a run of hits already under their belts. Pressure was applied to stop the British unit operating under the same name, so Jet Harris suggested the British band be known instead as the Shadows, the first real British pop band which went on to play a major part in rock 'n' roll history.

The first release to feature what came to be their own distinctive sound was in fact their fourth release, the instrumental *Apache*. The unusual clean, ringing guitar sound was produced by Hank playing a brand-new red Fender Stratocaster. The guitar was the first of its kind in the country, having been shipped over at the

RIGHT
Cliff Richard and Marty Wilde rehearse for 'Oh Boy' – note Rock and Roll footwear.

BELOW
Cliff and Marty and the 'Oh Boy' team – the late 1950s TV image of youth music in Britain.

ABOVE
Lonnie Donegan, who single handedly began the UK skiffle boom.

personal request of Cliff Richard. The record went on to become a massive hit, and was quickly followed by more in the same vein, including *Man of Mystery* and *FBI*. Their lack of a front man for their own act and their lazily choreographed dance steps, became an inspiration for a whole generation of aspiring British rockers.

But the man most responsible for the British groups of the early 1960s was perhaps the unlikely traditional jazzer Lonnie Donegan. Lonnie started as banjo player in Chris Barber's trad band and had a 15 minute slot in their sets in which he would play some 'skiffle'. Named after the jug bands of the 1920s, the music consisted mainly of simplistic covers of old Leadbelly songs.

A couple of skiffle tracks were recorded for a Chris Barber album in 1956 and, to everyone's surprise, they picked up a lot of radio airplay over the next few months on BBC programmes like *Housewives Choice* and *Worldwide Family Favourites*. This prompted Decca to release *Rock Island Line* as a single, credited to Lonnie Donegan and his Skiffle Band.

No one could have foretold the extent of the record's success. It went on to sell more than two million copies in the combined markets of the US and UK, a feat for which Donegan received just £50 from Decca – the basic Musicians Union rate at the time.

The appeal of Lonnie's skiffle lay in its accessibility. An old guitar or banjo, a washboard, a couple of thimbles and a one-string bass made from a tea chest and a broom handle meant anybody could have their own group. Hundreds sprang up all over the country, performing at church fêtes and street parties banging out a kind of British folk-blues. It was, in fact, the first participatory musical culture to hit Great Britain.

Although he also had many professional imitators only too willing to jump on the rolling bandwagon, Lonnie Donegan was alone at the head of his field. His career eventually included 27 British chart entries, but he too went the way of the all-rounder, with latter hits drawing on the traditional music hall novelty style with songs like *Does Your Chewing Gum Lose Its Flavour?* and the inimitable classic, *My Old Man's a Dustman*.

One of the many groups of youngsters that picked up on the skiffle craze were lads from Liverpool's Quarry Bank school. They called themselves the Quarrymen and one of their first shows was at the annual St Peter's Church garden fête in Woolton. On July 6, 1957, traditional songs like *Cumberland Gap* and *Maggie May* were given a skiffle airing with vocals and guitar courtesy of a young teddy boy called John Lennon.

Among the small crowd watching and listening was a confident young lad

ABOVE
Lonnie Donegan, whose later novelty hits should not detract from his earlier influential records.

dressed in a white drape jacket and tight black drainpipe trousers, who, at 15, was two years Lennon's junior. But what he lacked in age he more than made up for in ability.

James Paul McCartney gave the Quarrymen an unsolicited example of his skills, playing Eddie Cochran's *Twenty Flight Rock* note perfect, a reading of *Be Bop A Lula* which put the Quarrymen's earlier version to shame, and rounding off with an unnervingly accurate Little Richard impersonation. Lennon was impressed enough to ask McCartney to join the band and consequently a couple of weeks later they had a younger, more accomplished guitarist.

After playing a few more sporadic dates, the Quarrymen called it a day, although John and Paul, together with the even younger George Harrison, began to play wherever they could, under a succession of different names and with various drummers. Liverpool had a thriving local live music circuit at the time, with local dances out in the suburbs featuring five or six groups a night. The bills reflected the kind of music people wanted to hear, away from the formula-ridden sets to be found in the major city centre dance halls.

As inhabitants of one of Great Britain's biggest and busiest ports, Liverpudlians had access to a stream of import records arriving constantly from the United States. Almost everyone had a brother or a cousin who was a 'Cunard Yank' working the cross-Atlantic ships, so it was a relatively easy task to obtain copies of records that

RIGHT
The home-made appeal of skiffle was condoned by some unlikely reverential sources.

proved impossible to find in most other parts of the country.

The Liverpool music scene boasted a coterie of musicians who could acquire a new disc one day, rehearse it the next, and be playing it to a packed hall the day after. Of course, most of the crowd would think it was the band's own original material.

Because of the city's large number of proficient bands with a good knowledge of American music, Billy Fury returned to his home town to find a backing group for a tour. His manager, Larry Parnes, assembled most of the known groups and had them run through their paces, one of which was the Beatles, now settled with a name and featuring Lennon's friend Stu Sutcliffe on bass. However, they still lacked a permanent drummer and for this particular session were helped out by Johnny Hutchinson, whose normal position was behind the kit with local attractions the Big Three.

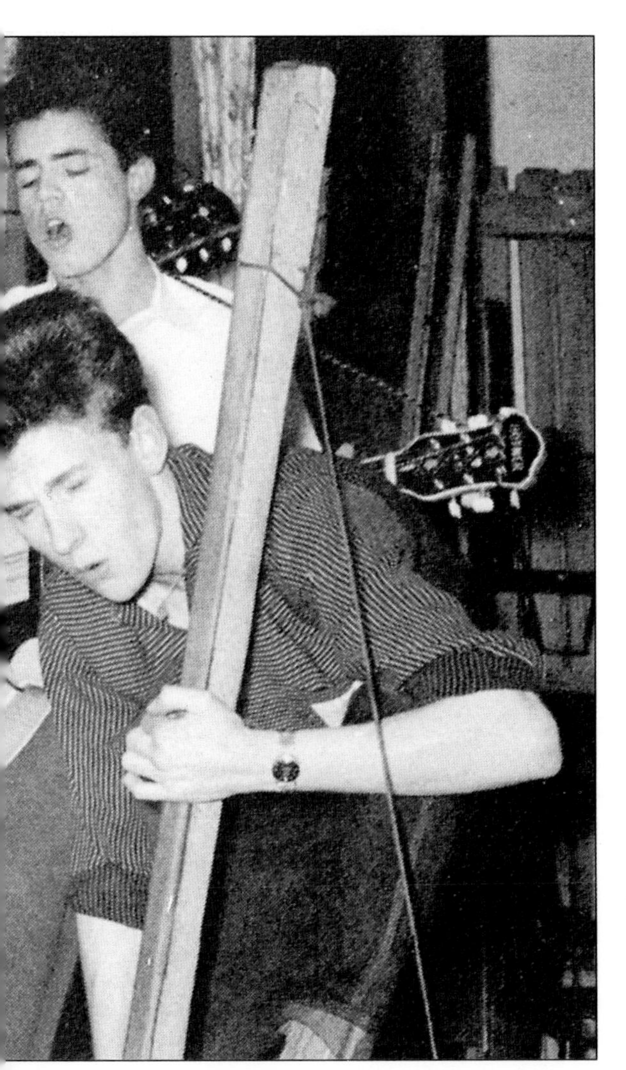

ABOVE
George Harrison, Stu Sutcliffe and John Lennon in the early days.

Despite the drummer's professional indifference, it was the Beatles who most impressed Billy Fury that day, much to their own surprise. The singer suggested to Parnes that the band be hired for the tour, which at the time was a very prestigious position, earning each musician as much as £100 per week. But very little escaped Parnes, and he saw through Sutcliffe's inadequacies as a bass player; the band was offered the tour but only if they replaced their artistically gifted though musically inept bass player. Lennon reacted with a typical burst of early arrogant leadership and told Parnes in no uncertain terms that it was all of the Beatles or none of them. Parnes settled on the latter.

But just one week later, Parnes gave the band the job of backing another of his singers, Johnny Gentle, on a tour of Scotland. For this first taste of life 'on the road', the Beatles received £5 a week each, except for Stu Sutcliffe who was paid nothing, so the band pooled their resources to include him. It was a perfect example of the camaraderie that stayed with the group throughout their touring career, and which enabled them to live through the experiences and pressures that the next few years would bring.

THE BRITISH ARE COMING 4

As the new decade, the 1960s, arrived, the music scene was firmly in the control of businessmen. With GI Elvis, the Reverend Little Richard and Chuck Berry's legally-enforced low profile clearing the way, the major labels unleashed a collection of clean-cut pop stars who were quite happy to toe the corporate line and sing innocent tunes from Tin Pan Alley and the Brill Building. Bobby Darin, Bobby Vee and the Everly Brothers were the 'boys next door', singing high school love songs which were as wholesome as home-cooked apple pie.

While Elvis was stationed in West Germany, RCA released a backlog of his material. At the time it was unusual for any artist to have recorded songs 'in the can', but Presley had cut a lot of sides before his conscription and the company had also acquired the rights to all the unreleased Sun sessions in their historic 1956 deal with Sam Phillips. From these recordings came the classic tearjerker *Old Shep*, which was the first song Presley performed in public, at a concert in his high school. Other tracks like *Big Hunk O'Love*, which went gold in 1959, kept a steady stream of singles in the charts and consequently maintained the high profile of the King.

When he was discharged from the armed forces in March 1960, many people waited with baited breath to see if two years' absence had sapped the Presley magic. The first fruit of his post army

BELOW
In later years John Lennon cynically claimed that Elvis died the day he joined the US army.

ABOVE
Elvis was demobbed by Washington, only to be conscripted by Hollywood and the US entertainment industry.

recording sessions was the 'comeback' single *Stuck On You*. It sold more than a million copies in six days, but was quickly pushed from the No. 1 position in the United States by the Everly Brothers, and in Great Britain was denied the coveted placing convincingly.

The sales and chart results would have been a remarkable success for any other act but for Presley it was a bitter disappointment. At the same time, Colonel Tom Parker was busy behind the scenes moving the King's career into wider family-based areas. When Elvis made an appearance on a Frank Sinatra TV special, swapping his army uniform for a dinner suit, many fans thought he had 'sold out' to the showbiz establishment that Sinatra personified. Effectively, Elvis had been discharged by the military only to be conscripted by the entertainment industry, with a posting to Hollywood where, much to Parker's delight, he could be assured of earning three million dollars a year for some nine weeks' work. For many it seemed that the popular youth

ABOVE
The Beatles finally stabilized their line-up, recruiting Pete Best on drums, and with McCartney moving to bass.

culture revolution led by rock 'n' roll was a thing of the 1950s, and that the new decade was to be dominated by the mainstream.

Around the same time that Elvis walked back onto civvie street, a young man called Pete Best joined the Beatles on the drummer's stool. Best was already known on the emergent 'beat' scene in Liverpool, mainly for his classic sultry good looks, cast in a James Dean mould, but also because his mother ran a popular music club in the expansive basement of their large suburban house.

Having at last finalized a stable line-up, the Beatles also acquired their first manager. Alan Williams ran one of the best-known clubs in the city, the Jacaranda, and it was through his contacts that the band came to play stints in Hamburg, thereby establishing some of the more enduring and sordid parts of their myth.

The month-long bookings at the Star club in the North German seaport forced the group to open up in many ways. Up until that time, they had been used to playing short half-hour sets, but in Hamburg were shocked to find that they were required to play for up to eight hours in one stretch. These marathon sessions had the effect of literally loosening the band up, with songs being extended into 20 minute jam sessions and the usually cool, staid composure onstage being replaced by a raucous, amphetamine-fuelled madhouse. John Lennon, in particular, rose to the occasion. In early displays of his anarchic and surreal humour, Lennon would often goosestep onstage, sometimes wearing a toilet seat around his neck, before going on to harangue the crowd with sardonic wit.

It was under these circumstances that a small group of German art students, including Klaus Voorman and his girlfriend Astrid, picked up on the strange group of leather-clad English rockers. Stu Sutcliffe's relationship with Astrid meant he eventually left the band to live with her in Hamburg, but not before she had imparted her distinctive hairstyle – with the swept-down fringe – to other members of the group.

When the Beatles returned to England after their final German trip, it was as a four-piece, with Paul McCartney on bass. A residency at the Cavern Club quickly established them as one of the most popular groups in Liverpool, and resulted in their link-up with Brian Epstein. Epstein came from a local business family and after several false starts ended up running the record-retailing side of the business. When the Beatles came to his attention, he immediately became enamoured enough with the band to offer to manage them.

The first thing Epstein did was to alter the group's image, introducing the high collar suits and generally tidying up the rocker image, before arranging demo audition sessions at most of the major labels in London. The most famous of these is the Decca session, which has been released in various unofficial and semi-legal formats. The Beatles taped their live set as a demo, but met with the same negative response from all the A&R men – the band was not good enough, had no good songs – with Decca even going so far as to say that guitar groups in general were finished.

A couple of months later, a disheartened Epstein once again made the journey to London with what was to be his final shot. He cut a couple of tracks to acetate and managed to sell them to a publisher, who in turn suggested Epstein should take

BELOW
Brian Epstein, George Martin and Gerry and the Pacemakers.

ABOVE
With the Beatles and Gerry and the Pacemakers, Brian Epstein controlled the two most successful groups in the country in 1963.

them to George Martin, who was a producer for the EMI subsidiary Parlophone.

Martin was impressed enough by the material to offer the group a deal, although he wanted to make some basic changes. Firstly he felt that the band should conform to the prevalent tradition of being called 'Someone and the Somethings', with Paul as the featured singer. This idea was firmly rejected by Epstein and the band, with Lennon particularly resenting the suggestion. Martin's second suggestion was that Pete Best was not up to standard, and should be replaced. Best was a popular figure, especially with the girl fans, and this may have been a factor in persuading other members of the band to go along with his dismissal. The dirty work was left to Brian, with the other Beatles shying away from facing Best themselves. The replacement was Ringo Starr, a colourful character who had crossed paths with the band many times as drummer with Rory Storm and the Hurricanes. Ringo quickly grew his quiff out into the Beatles' moptop style, but not before there were angry scenes from fans at the Cavern, demonstrating against Best's departure. At times, the atmosphere was electric, with George even receiving a black eye from one irate girl fan.

The result of the Beatles' first session with Martin was the single *Love Me Do* which reached number 17 in the national charts, due in no small part to the fact that Epstein's NEMS company was the largest distributor of records in the north of England.

A few months later in 1963, the Beatles were on their third tour of Britain, and their second single *Please Please Me* hit the number-one spot. Around this time, the fanatical screaming crowds of girls started to become a feature of their shows, and after an appearance at the London Palladium the fans' behaviour made front-page news, with a quick-witted sub editor coining the phrase 'Beatlemania'.

The end of the year saw 500,000 advance orders for *She Loves You* and a quarter-of-a-million advance for the album *With the Beatles*, beating the previous UK record holder Elvis Presley and his *Blue Hawaii* LP. With seven singles and EPs in the charts, the Beatles had achieved total domination of the British music scene.

The Beatles' campaign for the American market began in 1964. *From Me To You* and *She Loves You* sold reasonably well, but it was *I Want to Hold Your Hand* which made the band in the United States. The single took the all-important No. 1 chart position, selling more than 750,000 copies in the first three days. A couple of days later, the record was moving over the counters of New York shops to the tune of 10,000 copies every hour. By the beginning of February, *I Want to Hold Your Hand* had sold in excess of two million records, prompting Capitol, the band's US label, to initiate a $50,000 publicity campaign. To pave the way for the group's first Stateside visit, five million stickers were produced with the simple legend 'The Beatles are Coming'.

The four Beatles themselves were somewhat bemused by the American reaction. After all, they had basically stolen all they knew from US sources and so found it strange that they should be selling the ideas back to the people who had invented them.

Their arrival at Idlewild, now Kennedy Airport in New York later that month, surprised the band even more. More than 10,000 fans had gathered to welcome them with screaming demands for attention, waving placards saying 'Elvis Is Dead – Long Live Ringo' and 'Beatles For President'. The commotion was so great that Alec Douglas Hume, the current British Prime Minister, delayed his arrival for a day so as not to clash with the alternative British 'ambassadors'.

The press conference at the airport was a chaotic affair with over 200 reporters from TV and radio stations around the country. Murray 'the K' Kaufman, a disc jockey on Radio WINS, struck up an immediate rapport with George, which led to many subsequent exclusives and the tag 'the fifth Beatle'. The assembled hacks

BELOW
The Beatles, with Best's replacement Ringo Starr growing his rocker's quiff into a mop top style.

ABOVE
Lennon and McCartney giving Bob Dylan an endorsement.

could not believe their luck when they found four articulate young men who could run rings around the traditional list of stock questions. The Beatles came across as a kind of Marx Brothers, mixing rapid-fire witticisms with oblique surrealism, far from the more usual star and backing band eager to please a mainstream media.

After their triumphant arrival, the band were whisked off to the Plaza Hotel in the middle of New York, where the best part of a square mile of one of the world's busiest cities had been virtually sealed off by police to enable the four lads from Liverpool to remain unmolested by their fans. The band and their entourage occupied 10 rooms on the 12th floor of the plush hotel.

The main reason for their visit was a series of three appearances on the prestigious coast-to-coast Ed Sullivan TV show. The deal that Epstein concluded with Sullivan makes an interesting footnote to the later debate concerning his handling of the Beatles' financial affairs. Almost 10 years earlier, Elvis had received a $50,000 payment for a similar three-appearance package, without the benefit of the massive sales that the Beatles were enjoying. In stark contrast, Epstein had agreed on a payment of just $4,500 for each of the Beatles' sets.

Even so, their first performance on the show was something of a landmark in television history. Playing half a dozen songs, including *All My Loving* and *I Want to Hold Your Hand*, the Beatles came across as cool, collected customers in their first American live TV slot. Almost direct opposites to Presley's censored, sexually threatening image of a decade earlier, the Beatles' matching suits and clean shaggy haircuts looked almost asexual, and the band were perceived as little threat to the children of the land of the free. Viewing figures for the show made remarkable reading the next day – just under 74 million people had tuned in to watch the shock troops of what was soon to become a full-scale British musical invasion.

The band themselves were more worried about appearing in front of a couple of thousand fans in concert than performing before the unimaginable millions tuned in to the Sullivan show. So a warm-up show at the Coliseum in Washington DC provided their first taste of a live American audience. The screaming began the moment the band hit the stage, its intensity unlike anything the Beatles had previously experienced. It spurred them on to give a 100 per cent performance even though their backline Vox amps proved pitifully inadequate against the massed larynxes of thousands of highly excited teenage girls.

Two shows followed at the Carnegie Hall in New York, where the promoter assured Epstein that the tickets had sold so quickly he was sure he could have filled the massive Shea Stadium. The gigs were a re-run of Washington, with the hysterical crowd reaction going far beyond anything previously generated by Sinatra or Presley.

On their return to Britain, the Beatles were met like conquering heroes with another of what was to become a long line of overwhelming airport welcomes.

The American campaign had been a total success. For the taping of the final Ed Sullivan appearance, 50,000 people had applied for the 728 available seats. In the wake of the Beatles blitzkrieg, the next single *Can't Buy Me Love* had advance orders of over three million in the United States and Great Britain, and jumped straight into the No. 1 position in the singles charts on both sides of the Atlantic.

Back in England, the band completed their first feature film, *A Hard Day's*

BELOW
George Harrison and John Lennon on stage in the United States in 1964.

Night, and when they returned to the United States in August the same year, it was already showing at over 500 cinemas nationwide. The plan for their second visit was for the group to play live all over the country. The itinerary consisted of an exhaustive 32 shows in 24 different cities over a 33-day period. Wherever they went they were met with the same hysterical reactions, to the extent that, even when they took to travelling at night, thousands of fans would be awaiting them in the early hours of the morning. The devotion began to take on ridiculous extremes. After one interview carried an innocent reference to a penchant for jelly babies, the band found themselves inundated with the juvenile favourites whenever they set foot onstage. The tour climaxed with a spectacular show at Shea Stadium, where a capacity crowd of 55,000 screamed their way through the set and, in the process, gave the Beatles the highest gross for one show in entertainment history.

The level of crowd mania that the Beatles generated had not been seen before. The four were the most popular, and perhaps most famous, living people of the time. The extent of the situation led John Lennon to give an interview with

EVENING STANDARD THURSDAY AUGUST 4 1966

America's love affair with Beatles sours

Evening Standard Reporter

NEW YORK, Thursday.—America's love affair with the Beatles turned sour today as radio stations in several states banned their records in protest against alleged anti-religious remarks by John Lennon.

The announcers of a growing number of radio stations in cities and towns said they would follow the example of an Alabama station manager, Tommy Charles, who called for bonfires of their music and records across the nation.

However, announcers in some areas said they would continue to play Beatles' records, despite the furore which has arisen from a statement by John Lennon that the Beatles are more popular than Jesus, and that Christianity is on the way out.

[*The statement was made by John Lennon in an interview with Maureen Cleave which appeared in the Evening Standard and was reprinted in an American magazine.*]

Permanent ban

In Ogdensburg, New York State, Donald Ballou, general manager of the local station, said he had ordered the Beatles' songs banned permanently.

Ballou said: "I have personally read the article and do not appreciate my child listening to any group that would condemn Christianity. Neither would I allow my audience to listen to such a group."

A mobile Alabama station joined the Ban the Beatles movement, and the announcer said: "Lennon's statement is not only deplorable, but an outright sacrilegious affront to Almighty God."

'No bigotry'

In Conroe, Texas, the announcer said the Beatles had been banned but added: "We will re-consider if a public apology is made by a spokesman for the group."

However, the manager of the San Angelo, Texas, radio said: "We have taken them off and we don't care if they come out with 10,000 apologies, we will not play them again."

In Salt Lake City, programme director Bill Terry said: "I don't believe in religious bigots any more than I believe in Beatles bigots. I'm playing their records, not their religious ideals."

The campaign was joined last night by the Ku Klux Klan.

At Tupelo, Mississippi, Dale Walton, a Klan Grand Wizard, urged teenagers to "cut their wigs off" and send them to a "Beatle burning" being organised by the Klan on August 15.

● John Lennon is to desert the Beatles temporarily to star in a film on his own. The picture is called How I Won (the) War. Dick Lester, who directed the Beatles in their two films, will produce and direct this one

RIGHT

The frenzied receptions the Beatles received at airports the world over have since become legend.

BEATLES
OR
WELCOMES
THE BEATLES
KODAK SAFETY FILM
KODAK TRI X PAN FILM

Maureen Cleave of the London *Evening Standard* in which he said: 'Christianity will go, it will vanish and shrink. I needn't argue about that; I'm right and I will be proved right. We're more popular than Jesus now – I don't know which will go first, Christianity or rock and roll.'

When his remarks were printed in Britain, nobody took much notice, but in the United States, where the opinions of stars are held in higher esteem, it caused a massive furore. Tommy Charles, the manager of an Alabama radio station was the first to call for action, suggesting that listeners should send in their Beatles' records to fuel a vinyl bonfire. In Tupelo, Mississippi, the birthplace of Elvis, a Grand Wizard in the Ku Klux Klan called for teenagers to 'burn their wigs' and join in the condemnation. The affair was a tremendous setback for the band in America, tarnishing their cartoon-like image of innocence, and eventually leading to a humbling apology from Lennon before their next tour.

In August 1966, the Beatles again criss-crossed the country in what was to be the biggest-grossing, yet final, tour of their career. Not only were the ticket receipts massive but the merchandizing industry that had started two years before was still in full swing. At one point, the pillow cases they had used in one hotel were cut into 160,000 pieces and sold for $1.00 a time.

The Beatles' final live show took place in San Francisco on August 29, 1966. From that point onwards, the band was to explore new horizons opening up with the rapidly improving technology of the recording studio.

LEFT
The hysteria that greeted the Beatles on their US tours was on a scale never before seen.

RIGHT
A perk of fame is getting to meet your heroes. The Beatles are here seen with Mohammed Ali (then Cassius Clay).

SWINGING LONDON 5

The success of the Beatles' Stateside campaigns had far-reaching effects on the whole British music industry. From being a pale imitation of a shadow of American rock 'n' roll only a few years before, British music was now the infatuation of a generation of transatlantic youth.

The Beatles had smashed all previous record sales and concert attendance figures, and combined with their established merchandizing market, the financial turnover involved was far greater than that of Presley: a British accent alone was a saleable commodity in the United States.

John Peel, who was to become perhaps the most influential BBC DJ in the late 1960s and early '70s, had first-hand knowledge of this strange phenomenon. Known by his real name of John Ravenscroft at his first job at a radio station in Dallas, his accent was distinctly British. This simple fact caused the young and embarrassed Peel to be quite literally mobbed in supermarkets, and for the station to be inundated with calls for John to supply intimate information about the Beatles.

But the Beatles were not the only British artists winning the hearts and minds of young Americans; the floodgates had been opened and a tidal wave of musicians followed. Slowly but surely the spotlight shifted away from New York, Memphis, Nashville and Los Angeles to London, England, over 3,000 miles away.

In 1963, the staid sobriety of British society had been shaken to its foundations by the Profumo Affair. A number of highly-placed public figures, including cabinet minister John Profumo, were embroiled in a sex scandal which revolved around two young prostitutes, Christine Keeler and Mandy Rice-Davies. The impassive façade of pinstriped moralism was torn apart by these two unabashed, unrepentant goodtime girls. The incident was a pointer of things to come – the Britain of the 1950s was being left behind as a more liberated, youth-based culture began to take hold.

The Beatles were the first group to have their name and image commercially exploited, in a literal sense.

Up until this time, the word 'fashion' had been closely associated with the catwalks and parades of *haute couture*, an exclusive world to which ordinary people could only aspire. But in London, by the mid 1960s, the world of fashion was being turned on its head. Where once it had been led by highly-paid designers, the new impetus was now coming from streetwise, pill-popping, club-going teenagers.

Rock 'n' roll and 'pop' have always been linked with flamboyant dressing. From the loud, garishly electric colours of the early US stars, through the leather-clad 'rebel' rockers and up to the Beatles' edwardian elegance, the music world revolved around the maxim that 'clothes maketh the man'. In what was soon to be enduringly tagged

'Swinging London', dressing up became a national obsession.

Photographers of fashion themselves became stars, with Lord Lichfield and David Bailey, from different ends of the social strata, both embodying an 'Englishness' that was worth its weight in gold. The girls that they made famous were drastically different to the glamour models of the 1950s. In place of the curves of Mansfield and Monroe were the slimline, almost anorexic teenage frames of Twiggy and Jean Shrimpton. With their bobbed hair, eyes made big with mascara and pale lip gloss, they were the images of a whole new aesthetic, that of the high street superstar with accessible, affordable style.

London became a magnet for the new stylists. The hair salons of Vidal Sassoon, the consumer-orientated make-up products of Mary Quant, the photographic studios of Bailey and the op-art screenprint workshops of Bridget Riley, all were mixing and matching creative elements that were focused in the new world of pop culture.

In the music world, Brian Epstein had followed the earlier example of Larry Parnes and built up an impressive managerial stable of quality Liverpool groups. One of these, Gerry Marsden and the Pacemakers, were the first of the 'Merseybeat' wave to attain the No. 1 single slot. The song they took to the top was *How Do You Do It?,* which had originally been intended by George Martin for the Beatles' second single. The Beatles' version was so poor that it reinforced their argument for recording original material, but the tune was a great success for Gerry and the Pacemakers. It was convincingly followed by *I Like It* and *You'll Never Walk Alone*, both of which got to No. 1, and in so doing set a precedent which even the Beatles could not match and which was not equalled until 1984.

In the 'swinging London' of the mid-1960s, film, fashion, music and the art world collided in a chaotic, creative mix.

Epstein had many other successful acts on his books, including Cilla Black, who was frequently voted top female singer in music press polls, and Billy J Kramer, who never quite lived up to the Beatles' prediction that he would be 'the new Elvis'. But as well as the success of the Liverpool stars, the rough R&B sounds of Muddy Waters' Chess sides were among the records igniting sparks all over the country. From out of these embers grew a fully developed, though largely underground scene, based on rhythm and blues.

As early as 1962, Mick Jagger and keyboard player Ian Stewart featured in the Alexis Korner band. Korner was a gravel-voiced purist of the old school whose group was a training ground for many influential 1960s musicians. His own track record was extensive, but it was with his own band that he built up a devoted following in clubs such as London's Marquee.

Early in '62, Jagger met the strangely enigmatic Brian Jones. Jones, a year older than Jagger, was obsessed by the blues, especially the hard rhythms of the Chicago sound, and was musically gifted, quickly mastering the style on guitar. He also had a clear vision of the group he wanted to perform in – and lead – a raw, R&B energized collection of street-wise English white boys.

Jagger needed little persuasion to join him, with Stewart tagging along to become an unofficial member. Keith Richard, another devotee of R&B, joined the threesome while still attending Sidcup art

OPPOSITE LEFT
Mick Jagger on stage at the Crawdaddy Club in Richmond, a month before singing to Decca.

BELOW
Gerry Marsden, the first British artist to have his first three singles all become No.1's.

college. Together with a rhythm section of Charlie Watts and Bill Wyman, both of whom had served in Korner's ensemble, the group started playing the circuit.

Early dates were at the Marquee, standing in for Alexis Korner, at the Eel Pie Island Club, and at the Crawdaddy Club in the London suburb of Richmond. It was here that the newly-named Rolling Stones began to pick up attention. On Saturday 13 April, 1963, *The Richmond and Twickenham Times* carried a feature on one of the group's shows at the Crawdaddy at the Station Hotel.

ABOVE
Keith Richard, Brian Jones, Mick Jagger and Bill Wyman.

BELOW
The Rolling Stones's manager, ex-Epstein's office boy, Andrew Loog-Oldham.

By June that year, the group had acquired a manager, Andrew Loog Oldham, who had once been Brian Epstein's office boy. They also received their first national press exposure, with a piece in the *Daily Mirror*. Patrick Doncaster, 'the *Mirror's* DJ', was astounded by the Rolling Stones show: 'The guitars and drums started to twang and bang. Shoulder to shoulder on the floor stood 500 youngsters, some in black leather, some in sweaters. You could have boiled an egg in the atmosphere. They began to dance. And it was no place for Victor Silvester.' The photo which accompanied the article, showing the group scruffily scowling at the camera, reinforced the impression of five miscreants of dubious character. In the music paper *Melody Maker*, writer Ray Coleman made the same point as he asked:

'Would you let your sister go with a Rolling Stone?'

But by the end of the year, you simply would not have been able to stop her! The band's second single *I Wanna Be Your Man*, ironically penned by Lennon and McCartney, was their first big hit. It was followed by the even bigger success of *Not Fade Away*, which was also their first to scratch at the US charts. The Stones' material drew heavily from the music of Bo Diddley and Muddy Waters, but this time round it was being played by five lower middle-class white suburban Londoners who were managed by an ex-public schoolboy.

The press, however, presented quite a different image of the Rolling Stones. Most stories continued the earlier line of unkempt, undisciplined rebels, and their European tour of 1964 added fuel to the fire. At a Stones' show in the Hague, riot police halted the set after only 10 minutes due to disturbances in the crowd; in Paris, at the Olympia Theatre, there were more than 150 arrests; and in Blackpool the crowd caused £2,000 worth of damage to a venue, and Keith Richards was seen to kick a member of the audience in the eye.

There was more to come. In April, Jagger, Jones and Wyman were convicted of 'insulting behaviour' at a court in West London, and were fined £5 each – the charges arose from an incident in which the three had urinated in a petrol garage forecourt. The press had a field day, and they were not alone. The President of the National Federation of Hairdressers offered the band a free haircut, and went on record as saying that 'one of them looks like he's got a feather duster on his head', and a magistrate in Glasgow asked a 16-year-old fan up before him: 'What is the attraction for you with complete morons

ABOVE
The Rolling Stones take on the home of Merseybeat.

BELOW
The Stones in action on 'Ready Steady Go'.

like that? They have hair down to their shoulders, wear filthy clothes and act like clowns.'

But although their image as the 'bad boys' of British music continued to grow, the group achieved remarkable chart success. In late 1964 they started a run of five consecutive No. 1 singles: *It's All Over Now, Little Red Rooster, This Could Be The Last Time, (I Can't Get No) Satisfaction* and *Get Off My Cloud*.

It was *Satisfaction* that caught the imagination of a generation. While the establishment was trying to stifle the Stones – and by association, their fans too – the band articulated their simmering resentment and were consequently seen as a very real threat. But the level of success the group were enjoying meant the rewards came thick and fast. Charlie Watts was the first to initiate what was soon to become a stereotyped rockstar routine by buying a 16th-century country mansion in Sussex. The others soon followed suit, with Richards investing in Redlands, set amongst acres of Sussex countryside.

The hits kept coming; *19th Nervous Breakdown, Have You Seen Your Mother, Baby? Paint it Black*, and the well-received *Aftermath* LP. But, even so, the Stones were still seen as outsiders to the cosy industry, although by now some of their antics seemed little more than futile

ARDEN ENTERPRISES LTD. present

THE FABULOUS

EVERLY BROTHERS

BO DIDDLEY

with

'THE DUCHESS' & JEROME

THE ROLLING STONES

JULIE GRANT

MOST ☆ THE FLINTSTONES

Compere: BOB BAIN

29th, 6.00 & 8.30	DERBY, Gaumont	Fri., Oct. 11th, 6.30 & 8.45	BIRMINGHAM, Odeon	Thur., Oct. 24th, 6.45 & 9.00
1st, 7.00 & 9.10	DONCASTER, Gaumont	Sat., Oct. 12th, 6.15 & 8.30	TAUNTON, Gaumont	Fri., Oct. 25th, 7.00 & 9.20
2nd, 6.45 & 9.00	LIVERPOOL, Odeon	Sun., Oct. 13th, 5.40 & 8.00	BOURNEMOUTH, Gaumont	Sat., Oct. 26th, 6.15 & 8.30
3rd, 6.45 & 9.00	MANCHESTER, Odeon	Wed., Oct. 16th, 6.20 & 8.45	SALISBURY, Gaumont	Sun., Oct. 27th, 6.15 & 8.30
4th, 6.45 & 9.00	GLASGOW, Odeon	Thur., Oct. 17th, 6.45 & 9.00	SOUTHAMPTON, Gaumont	Tues., Oct. 29th, 7.00 & 9.30
5th, 6.15 & 8.45	NEWCASTLE, Odeon	Fri., Oct. 18th, 7.00 & 9.30	ST. ALBANS, Odeon	Wed., Oct. 30th, 6.45 & 9.00
6th, 5.45 & 8.00	BRADFORD, Gaumont	Sat., Oct. 19th, 6.20 & 8.45	LEWISHAM, Odeon	Thur., Oct. 31st, 6.30 & 8.45
8th, 7.00 & 9.10	HANLEY, Gaumont	Sun., Oct. 20th, 6.15 & 8.30	ROCHESTER, Odeon	Fri., Nov. 1st, 6.45 & 9.00
9th, 6.45 & 9.00	SHEFFIELD, Gaumont	Tues., Oct. 22nd, 6.30 & 8.45	IPSWICH, Gaumont	Sat., Nov. 2nd, 6.45 & 8.55
10th, 6.30 & 8.40	NOTTINGHAM, Odeon	Wed., Oct. 23rd, 6.15 & 8.30	HAMMERSMITH, Odeon	Sun., Nov. 3rd, 6.30 & 8.45

LEFT
The long-haired Rolling Stones in a 1964 publicity shot.

ABOVE
Promoters knew how to work artists in the mid-1960s.

RIGHT
The Beatles receive the MBE.

gestures. They finally appeared on the prestigious TV show *Sunday Night at the London Paladium*, but caused a row when they refused to take a bow with the other acts on the bill at the end of the show.

The Beatles had no such problems. A small industry had grown up around the band and, together with their cuddly cartoon image, it presented the shrewd Labour Prime Minister Harold Wilson with an excellent publicity opportunity. He included the four members of the band in the Queen's Birthday Honours list, awarding them the MBE. The silver medal of the Most Excellent Order of the British Empire, given personally by the Queen at Buckingham Palace. Some were outraged at the move, and a few war heroes returned their medals in protest, but on the whole it was accepted as a popular gesture.

The four Beatles went through their investiture at the Palace, with McCartney later commenting that the Queen had

ABOVE
Scooter runs to seaside resorts were a big part of the mod lifestyle, with Parkas and highly chromed Vespas and Lambrettas as prerequisites.

RIGHT
The Who, Ace Faces on the west London mod scene.

been 'very friendly' and 'she was like a mum to us all' – although in later years, Lennon would claim that they had all slipped off to the toilets to smoke a joint before meeting their sovereign, contrary to the perceived 'wholesomeness' of the group.

The Rolling Stones were not the only musical reaction to the Beatles, nor were they the only group on the emergent R&B scene. A whole new musical undercurrent was focussing on the material from the more recent Stax, Atlantic and, more importantly, Motown labels. The adherents of this new style called themselves modernists, or mods for short.

Mods had their own exclusive barbers, tailors, clubs and bands. They took great care and pride in their appearance, wearing the latest Italian fashions, three-button mohair suits and expensive Italian shoes, and had their hair in neat cuts that did not require handfuls of grease. Motor scooters, often customized with mirrors and chrome fittings, were their hallmark.

The Who were a group of West London lads that saw the value of affiliating to this emergent fashion and adopted a mod style. Roger Daltrey, Pete Townshend and John Entwhistle had been playing R&B sets around pubs in London's Shepherd's Bush, and picked up a small mod following. Keith Moon, a 16-year-old dedicated mod who was a manic drummer and wanted to join a band, decided the Who were to be the one.

Like Keith Richards, Pete Townshend was at art school. His arrogant attitude to his work was reflected in the importance of the visual arts in the Who's music. They wore loud mod fashions with a strong pop-art influence, and gained widespread interest in their live shows, where Townshend would trash his guitar among swirls of howling feedback, and Moon would demolish his drumkit and anything else he might find in his way.

Impressed by the speedfreak fury of the live sets and Townshend's songs, Peter Meadon took up management of the group. Changing the act's name to the High Numbers, Meadon wrote them a single, *I'm the Face* backed with *Zoot Suit*, which was released on Fontana. The record was not a great success, and in the aftermath Kit Lambert and Chris Stamp – brother of film star Terence Stamp – teamed up to take over the group's management and

have a PEPSI

BELOW
A highlight of a show by the Who was the ritual destruction of equipment. But even empty speaker cabinets cost something, and the pop-art symbolic violence quickly took the band into debt.

change their name back to the Who.

The group signed with Brunswick and released their first major single, *I Can't Explain*. Moon's demolition drumming sounds like a series of controlled explosions in a confined space, and distorted guitar riffs make *I Can't Explain* an inarticulate, confused noise – a true aural adrenalin rush.

The single reached No. 8 in the charts, and was followed by *Anyway, Anyhow, Anywhere*. This track was the first to utilize feedback creatively, although producer Shel Talmy remembers how the record company executives thought the noise was a mistake! But the innovative sounds failed to catch the imagination of the public, even though it was more representative of the band, and consequently its success was limited.

FAR RIGHT
The Who, catching a young audience.

The Who's third single, *My Generation*, stands as Townshend's finest moment but is also a millstone around his neck. The song was adopted as a theme for a generation, with the stuttering frustration of 'Why don't you all ffffffade away' and the eternal teenager's cry of 'I hope I die before I get old'.

With Paul McCartney tipping the Who as the biggest influence on pop music for 1966, and a string of TV appearances on shows like *Ready Steady Go*, which ended in equipment-smashing mayhem, Townshend was slipping into the role of spokesman for his fans. He held court in the music press, attacking the people who he thought were making music too complex or over-produced, and singling out Beach Boy Brian Wilson as 'living in a world of flowers, butterflies and strawberry-flavoured chewing gum. His world is nothing to do with pop. Pop is going out on the road, getting drunk and meeting the kids.'

But getting drunk and destroying their gear was costing the Who a small fortune, and in early 1966 the group switched labels to Reaction and released three more Top 5 hits: *Substitute, I'm a Boy* and *Happy Jack*. These records are clear examples of how the three-minute pop 45 was changing; Townshend's work was packed with well-drawn characters and pointed observations, a line in *Substitute* 'I was born with a plastic spoon in my mouth', a fine example of his sharp mind.

Ray Davies was a contemporary of Townshend and, alongside his brother Dave Davies, formed the heart of the Kinks. The band had typical origins for the time, playing R&B at debutantes' balls in 1963 under the name of the Ravens. Early in 1964 they changed their name and signed to the Pye label.

Their first single, a version of Little Richard's *Long Tall Sally*, owed much to the Beatles' take of the song but neither it nor their second, *You Do Something To Me,* made an impression on the charts or public. It was their third effort, the first to be written by Ray Davies, that hit home. *You Really Got Me* has the same forceful slabs of guitar that open *I Can't Explain*, in this case the sound being achieved by poking holes in the amplifier speakers with a pencil! The almost deadpan vocal delivery was heavily at odds with the histrionics of the Who's Daltrey, but the

overall power of the track burst out unchecked.

The group cultivated an image of sartorial elegance, often appearing in ruffed, lace shirts and sometimes in full 'horse and hounds' hunting season outfits. The United States quickly took to this familiar, although slightly askew, British caricature, but Davies was in fact writing about his own position on 'Swinging London'. His thoughts and opinions on the subject can be found in the words to *Well Respected Man* and *Dedicated Follower of Fashion*, both hits in 1966. The sardonic, cynical tone was perhaps missed by the many who bought the cheerfully chirpy tunes, but Davies made it quite clear to all who wished to know that he was not at home in the social swirl of the London scene.

LEFT
The Kinks, featuring brothers Ray and Dave Davies.

BELOW LEFT
The Small Faces – their mod image was not a pose, but a way of life.

BELOW
The Small Faces created a musical marriage of credible soul influences and a classic British pop sensibility.

The Who adopted a mod stance, and the Kinks were on the trend's periphery, but one group which truly grew out of the mod scene was the Small Faces. Ronnie Lane was an 'ace face', one of the sharpest dressers, the coolest stylists. His friends, Kenny Jones and Steve Marriot, wore the same clothes, went to the same clubs, danced to the same music and took the same pills, and their first single, *Whatcha Gonna Do About It*, was released a few months after the Who's debut.

The record got to No. 14 in the charts, and was quickly surpassed by the follow-up *Sha La La La Lee* which went up to No. 3. Ian McLagen joined on keyboards, and Marriot and Lane started to record their own songs. With *Hey Girl*, *My Mind's Eye* and the magnificent *All or Nothing* all reaching the Top 10, the band achieved a synthesis of pop sensibility and rough R&B that was both sweet enough for the charts and credible too.

But by this time the mods were hitting the headlines for less palatable reasons. Each Bank Holiday, hundreds of young mods made pilgrimages to seaside resorts, often in convoys of Vespa and Lambretta scooters, and towns such as Brighton and Bognor saw fierce clashes with groups of 'rockers' – leather-clad bikers with a traditional taste in rock 'n' roll. The battles

on the beaches made front-page news. Riot squads of specially equipped police were flown to the scenes to contain the trouble and special sittings of courts were held to deal with offenders. Featured press pictures showed British youths mercilessly beating others, and caused widespread revulsion and comment. Asked for his opinion of the disturbances, and whether he was a mod or a rocker, Ringo Starr replied: 'I'm a mocker'.

Late in 1966, a young Italian film director, Michelangelo Antonioni, shot his film *Blow Up* in and around London. Said to be based on the life of David Bailey, the film stars David Hemmings as a young, successful photographer who becomes entangled in a psychological drama which revolves around a character played by Vanessa Redgrave. The wild merry-go-round social whirl of London in the mid-1960s is captured perfectly, with Hemmings moving from one set of ambitious models to the next, from his fashionable mews studio/flat to the equally desirable environs of antique shops.
A typical club scene in the film has the Yardbirds, featuring Jeff Beck and Jimmy Page, playing live on stage.

The Yardbirds had been formed in 1963 by Keith Relf, Chris Dreja and Paul

ABOVE
The arch-enemies of mods – the motorbiking rockers.

Samwell-Smith. Together with Jim Carty on drums, they played raw R&B on the club circuit of Eel Pie Island, the Crawdaddy and the Marquee. It was at the Marquee, in London's Wardour Street, that they recorded the seminal *Five Live Yardbirds*, with Eric Clapton on guitar. Clapton was gifted, and passionate about his playing. His style was a heavily amplified version of black blues' players like BB King and Albert King, fluid lead runs based around his own belief that 'it's not what you play, it's what you leave out that counts'.

By 1965, the band had a hit with *For Your Love*, but shortly afterwards Clapton left to join John Mayall's Bluebreakers, looking for a stricter blues' line. His replacement was Jeff Beck, suggested by top session player Jimmy Page and the perfect choice. His Fender Esquire supplied clean cutting breaks, mixing traditional blues' runs with the poppier lines of *Heartful of Soul, Still I'm Sad, Shapes of Things* and *Over Under Sideways Down*, which were all hits in 1966. When Dreja moved on to bass, Page joined on guitar, this line-up produced the *Blow Up* band which featured two of the greatest guitar heroes of all time.

LEFT
The Yardbirds, whose ranks at various times included Eric Clapton and Jimmy Page, here pictured with Jeff Beck on guitar.

BACK IN THE USA

But while much of the world's attention was centred on the British music scene, the United States was busy producing its own uniquely American superstars.

The very early 1960s saw a boom in a West Coast sound based on that most traditional of Californian pastimes – surfing. Tunes like *Wipeout*, and acts like Jan and Dean, took the happy-go-lucky songs to the top of the charts all over the world, but the only group to come out of the craze and have any lasting impact on rock and pop music was the Beach Boys.

Dennis, Carl and Brian Wilson were three brothers skilled in singing 'barber shop' accapella (unaccompanied) close harmonies. Their father, Murray, who was to become their manager, was a professional songwriter, and arranged for his boys to get together with their cousin Mike Love, who had written a song called *Surfin*. After cutting a demo, they ended up with a sizeable local hit, and having joined up with family friend Al Jardine on guitar, they signed to Capitol records.

The group were a classic example of being in the right place at the right time. Clean cut, all-American white boys, products of a system that meant many 15-year-olds owned their own cars, their music was devoted to surfing; the boards, the buggies, the beaches and, of course, the girls.

Almost a mirror opposite of the Beatles – where the Liverpool lads wore leathers against the harsh Hamburg winters, the Wilsons wore shorts and T-shirts for the beach; where the British foursome talked in an exaggerated working-class 'scouse', the American five-piece spoke in a laid-back Californian drawl – both bands were playing souped-up Chuck Berry songs mixed with syrupy ballads. The Beach Boys' Berry influence was undeniable. *Surfin' USA* is simply *Sweet Little Sixteen* with different words; *Fun Fun Fun* is its twin brother, even down to the opening licks. But the thing that made their treatments stand apart was the use of the soaring harmonies and crystal-clear voices.

The band rivalled the Beatles in both sales and popularity. Even when the surf music scene had all but dried up, the group kept on having hits like *Surfer Girl*. But *All Summer Long*, released in 1964, turned out to be the Beach Boys last surf-based album. Even though it spawned tracks like the double million seller *I Get Around*, Brian Wilson had already decided to move on.

RIGHT
The Beach Boys, left to right – Al Jardine, Bruce Johnston, Dennis Wilson, Mike Love, Carl Wilson.

BELOW
The cover of the seminal 'Pet Sounds' album – said to be the inspiration for 'Sgt. Pepper'.

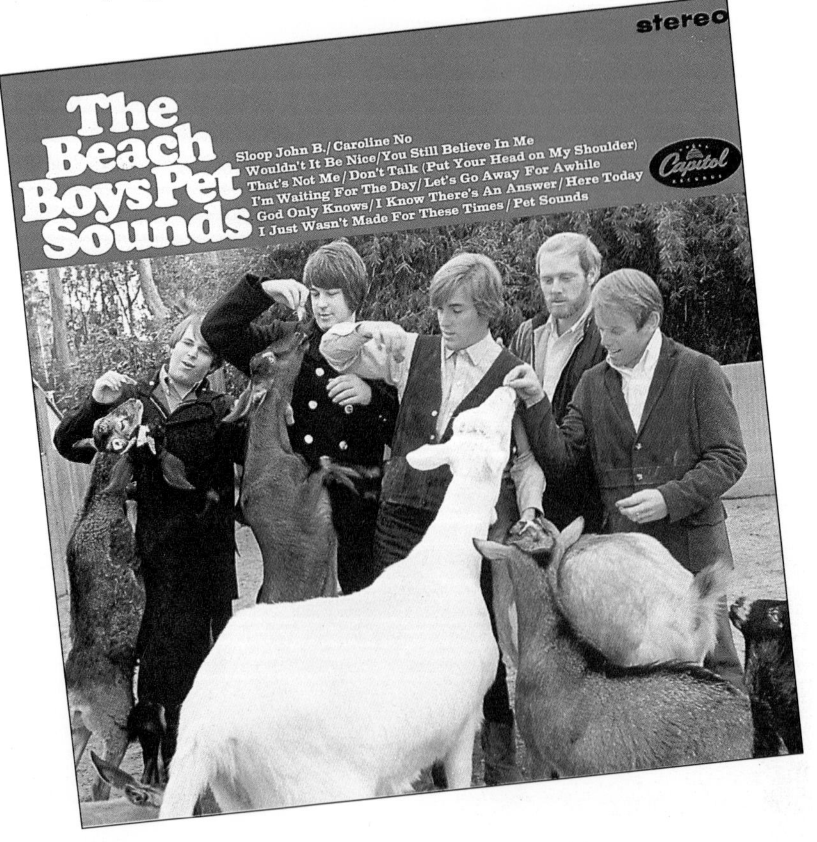

Brian was by now well established as the creative force of the group. He wrote most of the songs, many in conjunction with Mike Love, but, more importantly, he arranged and produced the records, sculpting the voices into pictures of sound. After *All Summer Long* Brian took a year off, amid rumours of his massive drug intake, but out of the tales of musical madness came the seminal album *Pet Sounds*. Although his mind may have been in chaos, Brian's music was sweet. Songs like *God Only Knows* and *Caroline No*, later released as a Brian Wilson solo single, show the writer at the height of his powers. It is widely believed that an advance copy of the album acted as the spur for Paul McCartney to initiate the *Sergeant Pepper* sessions.

The Beach Boys were the sound of the West Coast, but in New York the music scene was based around a folk culture establishing itself in the bars and coffee houses of Greenwich Village.

A whole host of singers did the rounds on the small but influential circuit, many owing much to the style of the semi-legendary Woody Guthrie – but the old, dying singer reserved his own endorsement for a wild hillbilly called Bob Dylan.

LEFT, RIGHT AND FAR RIGHT Three of the many faces of Bob Dylan.

Dylan had been Robert Zimmerman, in Minnesota, in 1941. As a youth he had taken piano lessons, and played in a few rock 'n' roll bands – even backing Bobby Vee on some dates (he was sacked!) – and attending Minnesota University. In 1959 he dropped out, started hanging around in beatnik circles, and adopted the name Dylan, and by 1961 he was living in Greenwich Village, mainly crashing on friends' floors. Playing any venue that he could, his hard style soon won him a growing reputation, and his arrogant self-belief and passionate delivery set him apart from other, more middle-class liberal hipsters.

Journalist Robert Shelton ran a piece on Dylan in the *New York Times* in 1962. He had witnessed a set at Gerdes and liked what he saw, and a deal with CBS followed shortly. Dylan's first album for the label cost less than $500 to make, a collection of blues' standards by the likes of Blind Lemon Jefferson, and traditional songs like *House of the Rising Sun*. There were also two of Dylan's own numbers, one a tribute to Guthrie, and both in a basic 12-bar format.

It was his second album that opened many people's eyes. *The Freewheelin' Bob Dylan* was released later that year, and was entirely original material. *Blowing in the Wind, A Hard Rain's A Gonna Fall, Masters of War* and *Talkin' World War III Blues* are all included on the LP. The words, powerful and certainly political, contained stream-of-consciousness images of floods, wars, politicians and nuclear bombs which were a million miles away from the normal teen angst love formula. Dylan's challenging stance and openly intellectual ideas were an innovation, and one that left the Beatles' witty ironies looking less credible and rather irrelevant.

Known mainly for performance, the fact that the likes of Peter, Paul and Mary were covering Dylan's *Blowing in the Wind* meant he was gaining recognition as a writer. When he appeared at the Newport Folk Festival in 1964, it was as a virtual unknown, a long way down the bill. When he returned at the end of the event to lead the assembled headliners through a version of *Blowing in the Wind*, he was already being acclaimed as the new star of the folk movement.

His third album, *The Times They Are A Changin*, became a worldwide hit, but on tour later that same year, Dylan drastically cut the amount of his older, 'protest' material in the set, and replaced it with songs based around his view of 'relationships'. Nonetheless, Dylan continued to challenge the established order, saying that lifelong love was a self-evident impossibility:

You say you're looking for someone
Who'll pick you up each time you fall,
A lover for your life and nothing more
Well, it ain't me babe.

It Ain't Me Babe

Predictably, the fans did not like the shift of emphasis, and attacked Dylan for making it. It wasn't the last time he was to find himself at odds with his audience.

At Newport in 1964 he had performed a song called *Mr Tambourine Man*, once again pipping everyone to the post – Dylan had written the first 'drug' song, although that fact went unnoticed by most who heard it. But it was when he returned to headline the festival the following year that Dylan caused his biggest rumpus. He walked onstage carrying an electric guitar and, backed by most of the Paul Butterfield Blues Band, launched into a searing version of *Maggie's Farm*. This was quickly followed by *Like A Rolling Stone*.

The folk fans objected. Dylan, their spokesman, had taken their safely radical faith, ripped it up and thrown it back at them. Amid boos and catcalls and shouts of 'cut the wires', he returned to the stage alone with an acoustic guitar. In his inimitable snarl he sang to the crowd *It's All Over Now Baby Blue*.

In August, *Highway 61 Revisited* was released, including among its tracks *Like A Rolling Stone* and *Desolation Row*. With a permanent backing group known as The Band, Dylan undertook a world tour with his electric set. In the United States and Australia he suffered extremely mixed receptions, and in Great Britain people walked out of the shows all over the country. The tour ended at the Royal Albert Hall in London where Dylan was confronted with shouts of 'Judas'. The truth was that he was moving too fast for his audience to follow.

Then, in July 1966, came the news that Bob Dylan had been involved in a serious motor bike crash in New York State. Out of the many rumours that surfaced, the facts appeared to show that he had broken vertebrae in his neck, with the result that he quite simply disappeared for the next two years. There was a complete blackout of information and contact between Bob Dylan and the outside world.

In the meantime, the effects of the British invasion led by the Beatles continued to filter through the US music scene. In Greenwich Village, a 1964 sign outside a bar read: 'Jim McGuinn – Beatle impressions'. Jim later became Roger, and, together with Gene Clark, David Crosby and Chris Hillman, formed the Jet Set. All were regulars on the acoustic folk scene, but as McGuinn later explained: 'I saw this gap, with the Beatles and Dylan leaning towards each other in concept. That's where we aimed.' The band signed a one-record deal with Elektra, and released a single under the dreadful name, the Beefeaters.

Soon afterwards, however, they signed to Columbia and became the Byrds. The British group the Animals had already had hits with workings of Dylan arrangements, and so it was suggested that the Byrds record a version of *Mr Tambourine Man*. Six months later, when the single was eventually released, it reached the top of both the US and British charts. It was a sublime moment in the merging of rock and pop music. A drug song written by an

BELOW
The Byrds, featuring Mike Clark, Gene Clark, David Crosby and Roger McGuinn.

ABOVE
The Byrds took Dylan's approach and merged it with the Beatles, culminating in the classic 'Mr Tambourine Man'.

'angry young man' folk poet, played by a country-folk group obsessed by the Beatles – with the end result being three minutes of classic mid-1960s pop.

Throughout the rest of 1965 the group followed up with *All I Really Want To Do* and *Turn! Turn! Turn!*, fulfilling their role as popstars for screaming kids, but quickly becoming disillusioned with the gold at the end of their rainbow. Inwardly they yearned to be recognized as 'serious' musicians.

The last thing that Bert Schneider and Robert Rafelson wanted was serious musicians. They placed an advertisement reading 'Madness!! – auditions: folk and rock musicians/singers for acting roles in new TV series – running parts for four insane boys, age 17–21.' in *Variety* magazine hoping to find four players for their new TV show, which was to feature the adventures of 'an unknown, young, long-haired modern-dressed group and its dreams on the way to fame and fortune'.

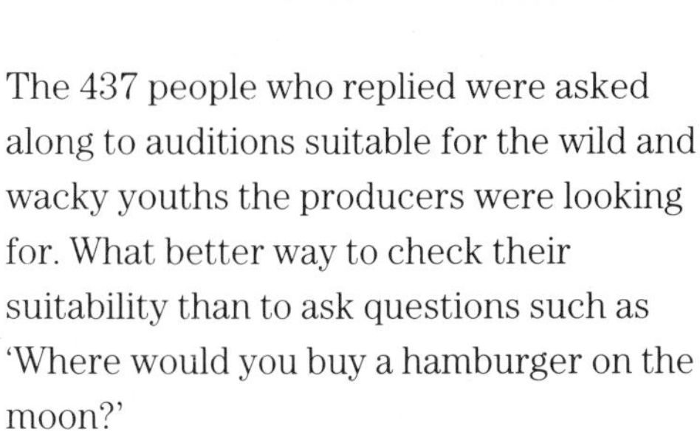

The 437 people who replied were asked along to auditions suitable for the wild and wacky youths the producers were looking for. What better way to check their suitability than to ask questions such as 'Where would you buy a hamburger on the moon?'

Mickey Dolenz was the first to pass the test. Faced with a stack of Coke bottles he stared at them for a few moments before moving one slightly and declaring 'Checkmate!' He was soon joined by Peter Tork, a veteran of the Village folk circuit; Davy Jones, a cockney with a couple of US singles under his belt and a fan club several thousand strong; and Mike Nesmith, who was the closest of the four to being a serious musician.

The musical side of the venture was seen strictly as a promotional device. A single, *Last Train to Clarksville*, was released in the hope of picking up some radio publicity for the TV show. By the time the first of the series was screened in September 1966, the record was already in the Top 100. Two months later it was No. 1 selling more than a million copies. The hastily released album stayed at the top

BELOW
The Monkees in typically wacky pose.

slot for 15 weeks, putting the Monkees in the same bracket as the Beatles in terms of sales.

The TV series itself was slow to pick up viewers. At first it was not even broadcast nationwide. But with the success of the records and the skilful scripts of the team behind the *Dick Van Dyke Show* it soon began to draw good audiences. By now the charts provided an easy target. The end of the year saw *I'm a Believer*, written by Neil Diamond, soar to the top of the charts all around the world. The group even toured to great screaming receptions, although they soon suffered a backlash when it was 'revealed' that they did not actually play on their own records.

Whereas the Monkees were a fine example of (pop) art imitating life and the epitome of the calculated, business-based star-maker approach, in Detroit Berry Gordy Jnr set up a hit factory around more informal, family-like ideals. By the time he was in his mid-30s Gordy had run a record shop that had gone bankrupt, dabbled in boxing, had been a songwriter, and ran a publishing company that released tracks through Chess. 1960 saw him give up a job on a Detroit car production line and, with a borrowed $600 launch his own record label. He called it Tammie, though it was soon changed to Tamla.

The first group Gordy signed was the Miracles, whose work he had already produced. The label's first hit was *Money*, recorded by Barret Strong and written by Gordy himself. The track had been recorded at the Chess/Checker studios and originally released by Gordy's sister on her own Anna records label. It was quickly transferred to Tamla, and was a big hit.

One of Gordy's main aims was to reach out beyond the limited black record market. He had seen how labels like Chess and Stax ran effectively to a small sector, but he saw the chance of a crossover to mainstream white audiences and he launched a range of labels under the overall banner of Motown.

The hits started coming. The Miracles, led by Smokey Robinson and his silky voice, had success with *Shop Around* and *You've Really Got a Hold On Me*. The Marvellettes gave Motown its first No. 1 with *Please Mister Postman* in 1961. But

INSET, BELOW RIGHT
Berry Gordy Jnr. in 1964

OPPOSITE PAGE
The Monkees were the ultimate exercise in commercial art imitating life, 'with hilarious consequences'.

BELOW
Smokey Robinson and the Miracles. Smokey was in many ways the lynchpin of the company in the early years.

the first to achieve Berry's real aim was a 12-year-old blind boy called Little Stevie Wonder. He had been introduced to the boy and at once recognized his incredible potential – apart from having true musical skills Stevie also had a very good sympathy-selling angle. He was launched as a kind of young Ray Charles, and had a hit with the live recording *Fingertips*, the first Motown record to be in the R&B chart and the Top 100 at the same time.

Berry Gordy had wanted to be seen as running a successful, modern American company with universal appeal while maintaining a definite black identity. With his empire including the publishing house Jobette, and its various labels Tamla, Motown, Gordy, VIP and Soul, he had achieved his goal.

The companies were based in three converted houses on Grand West Boulevard. There was a regular house band, and with Smokey Robinson writing for and producing the Temptations, the general atmosphere was worklike but informal. Gordy made sure his records were aimed at whites as well as blacks, and the productions took into account details like how the records sounded on jukeboxes.

Martha Reeves was a secretary for the Corporation in 1961. When some backing singers were quickly needed for a Marvin Gaye session, Martha volunteered. She and her friends began regular studio work, eventually releasing their first single as Martha and the Vandellas in 1963 with *Come and Get Those Memories*. It was followed by *Heatwave, Dancing in the Street* and *Jimmy Mack*. It was a perfect example of the 'in-house' informal success of Motown. Marvin Gaye himself was the first major Motown star. His voice, steeped in years of gospel singing, invokes shivers with the almost religious zest of *Can I Get a Witness?*. Together with Smokey Robinson these acts represented the first phase of Motown.

LEFT
Early Motown stars The Temptations.

OPPOSITE PAGE
Stevie Wonder was discovered by Berry Gordy, who coached his talents with incredible results.

BELOW
Martha and the Vandellas were a perfect example of the 'in house' Motown approach, leading to a long string of worldwide hits.

ABOVE
Diana Ross (left) and the Supremes were the stars of Motown's second wave, coinciding with the arrival of writing team Holland, Dozier, Holland.

OPPOSITE PAGE
The Four Tops were responsible for many of what are now seen as classic Motown tracks.

RIGHT
Marvin Gaye was perhaps Motown's first true star, and an undeniable influence on many later singers.

At an extraordinary board meeting in 1964, Berry Gordy Jnr. announced that Smokey Robinson was to become vice president of the Motown Corporation, but due to his work with both the Miracles and the Temptations, as well as writing for other artists – *My Guy* for Mary Wells, for example – Smokey was unable to take up the post until 1972.

Motown's second wave coincided with the arrival of the remarkable songwriting team of Eddie Holland, Lamont Dozier and Brian Holland. Writing songs for the Supremes, the Four Tops and the Isley Brothers, they notched up an incredible list of hits: *Where Did Our Love Go?*, *Baby Love*, *This Old Heart of Mine*, *Reach Out I'll Be There*, *Bernadette* and many others. Their writing captured a special quality that allowed Motown to tag itself 'The Sound of Young America'. The Four Tops had further hits with *Baby I Need Your Loving* and *The Same Old Song*, and the Supremes had 15 successive top 10 hits. Motown had stamped out its own clear identity: at its height in the mid-1960s, it was possible to write to Motown from anywhere in the world by simply addressing a letter to: 'Hitsville, USA'.

LOVE AND WAR 7

In the late 1950s, the Haight Ashbury district of San Francisco had been colonized by beatniks. The area, bounded by Haight Street and Ashbury Street, had a bohemian atmosphere, so much so that at the time it was said that 'even the cops don't wear bullet proof vests'.

Writer Ken Kesey had settled there at the beginning of the decade, and by the mid-1960s he was living comfortably off the royalties of his book, *One Flew Over The Cuckoo's Nest*. He was also one of the first people to be converted to the cause of

ABOVE
Examples of the surreal and esoteric art images that grew up around the drug-based 'deadhead' culture.

Lysergic Acid Diethylamide 25, more commonly known as LSD or 'acid'.

Kesey was a firm believer in the life-changing properties of LSD. He saw the drug as a mental key that literally opened doors of perception, giving the user experience of different planes of reality. By 1965 he was at the centre of a loose grouping of like-minded souls who became collectively known as 'The Merry Pranksters'. Amongst their numbers was Neal Cassady, who had been the model for Jack Kerouac's seminal beat novel, *On the Road*.

The Pranksters' mission was to spread the word of acid revelation, and, to this end, they bought a brightly painted bus and set off around the country on the journey that Tom Wolfe documents in the *Kool Aid Acid Test*. Back in Haight Ashbury, the group held large parties, where many of the drinks were heavily spiked, and it was through these sessions that Augustus Owsley Stanley III came on the scene.

Owsley was a chemical genius and was the man behind the first mass production of LSD, which was at the time still perfectly legal. He also had a circle of friends who formed a group, the Grateful Dead, and often oversaw their live sound.

The Dead, soon entrenched in the Pranksters' acid circle, appeared at an event called the Trips Festival organized at the Longshoreman's Hall in the Bay and the first of many 'happenings'. With the

BELOW
The Grateful Dead on stage at Madison Square gardens, with Jerry Garcia on the left.

ABOVE
The talented, sardonic Frank Zappa.

OPPOSITE PAGE
Jefferson Airplane, featuring Grace Slick, Paul Katner and Marty Balin.

long set of the Dead featuring their growing, riff-based extended jams, highlighted by the psychedelic light show, the festival was a wild success.

By the end of 1966, the Bay area of San Francisco was the mecca of a rapidly expanding 'hippie' movement, with Jerry Garcia and Bob Hunter leading the Haight Ashbury 'deadheads'. Acid was not the first drug to fuel a whole new sound; Charlie Parker and Miles Davies had launched their exploratory stabs in modern jazz using morphine, and British groups had widely used amphetamines, but the consciousness-expanding LSD was seen as a wider threat.

Acid was at the heart of the hippie philosophy. 'Turn on, tune in and drop out' ran a popular phrase of the time, and the whole ethos questioned and challenged the accepted capitalist way of life. To complicate matters, the US had just committed itself to a growing involvement in the Vietnamese war.

Frank Zappa and his band, the Mothers of Invention, openly flaunted the law by appealing to young American men to ignore the Vietnam draft. Zappa (his real name) was an accomplished musician whose band merged a number of complicated styles into a unique formula. A barely hidden streak of vicious irony runs through most of his work, which was very political.

But Zappa soon realized the futility of taking on the role of spokesman for hippie culture. His 1967 album, *We're Only in it For The Money*, was a cynical expression of his views on the assimilation of hippie values with business concerns.

The first of the Bay area groups to achieve national recognition was Jefferson Airplane. Paul Kantner and Marty Balin named their group after a legendary blues singer, Blind Lemon Jefferson, in 1965. They were at the centre of a circle of musicians which included members of Moby Grape, Quicksilver Messenger Service and several others. After a few false starts they quickly settled on a line up that included Grace Slick on vocals.

The band was openly inspired by the Byrds and, with their roots firmly in the folk scene, they were aiming at the same folk/pop crossover. They signed a deal with RCA Victor for a $20,000 advance, and released *White Rabbit* as their second single. *White Rabbit*, clearly a drug song, was an instant success around the world, with Slick's tempestuous vocals driving the song to its swirling climax.

By the summer of 1967 a whole alternative hippie culture had grown up. Clothes were worn loose-fitting, with brightly coloured patterns and beads and bangles, hair outgrew social conventions,

with even the Beatles sporting beards and moustaches, and flowers were the sign of the times. Peace and love were *the* buzzwords.

Underground press titles *International Times* and *Oz* allowed new writers, such as Charles Shaar Murray, to talk of drugs, politics and the Rolling Stones, and the creators of *Fritz The Cat* and *The Furry Freak Brothers*, Robert Crumb and Gilbert Shelton, had their work treated as subversive literature.

But in spite of all this, the hippies did not take a political stance within the system. Just as many of its elder statesmen had background histories of left-wing involvement, many of its younger members went on to become extremely successful in the capitalist sphere. Nonetheless the counter-culture challenged the concept of lives spent on a 9–5 working treadmill, and many started to look inwards for fulfilment.

In 1967, the Monterey Pop Festival was held in California. It was the first of a string

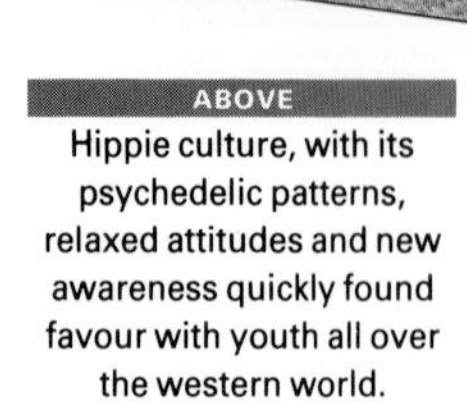

ABOVE
Hippie culture, with its psychedelic patterns, relaxed attitudes and new awareness quickly found favour with youth all over the western world.

of events that would eventually become synonymous with both the hippies and their 'New Age'. John Phillips and Lou Adler organized the event, which attracted over 30,000 customers, and was the first bill of its kind to feature a strict diet of rock acts. Eric Burdon and the Animals and the Who appeared from Britain, and Jefferson Airplane and Janis Joplin showed the direction of American West Coast rock.

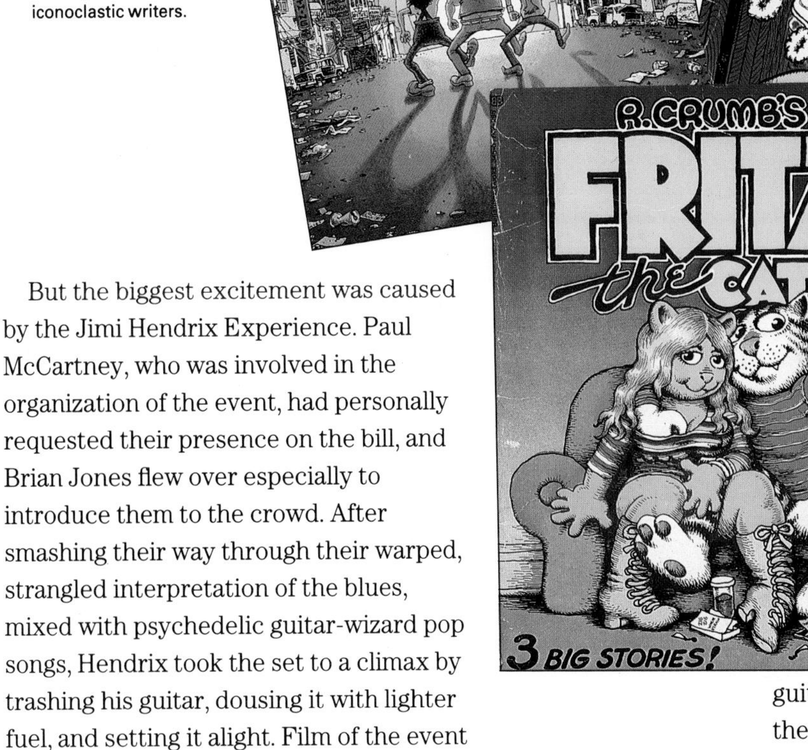

RIGHT
Crum's and Shelton's comic masterpieces stand the test of time, and magazines like Oz were a fertile breeding ground for a new generation of iconoclastic writers.

But the biggest excitement was caused by the Jimi Hendrix Experience. Paul McCartney, who was involved in the organization of the event, had personally requested their presence on the bill, and Brian Jones flew over especially to introduce them to the crowd. After smashing their way through their warped, strangled interpretation of the blues, mixed with psychedelic guitar-wizard pop songs, Hendrix took the set to a climax by trashing his guitar, dousing it with lighter fuel, and setting it alight. Film of the event shows Hendrix lovingly caressing the burning, howling instrument, before violently smashing it again and again.

But Hendrix had been no overnight success. After leaving national service in 1963, during which he had volunteered for the Parachute Regiment, he went on the road backing various artistes on tour, including Little Richard, Ike and Tina Turner, Wilson Pickett and the Isley Brothers.

In 1965 he formed his first group, Jimmy James and the Blue Flames, and was seen by many famous people, including the Beatles, the Stones and Bob Dylan, playing sets at the Café A Go Go in New York. Word about the manic style of the young black guitarist quickly spread. Chas Chandler, the bass player with the Animals (who were on the verge of splitting up) had already made the move into management and production, and persuaded Hendrix to accompany him back to Great Britain, on the strength of a promised meeting with Eric Clapton.

London was the hub of the world's music industry when Hendrix arrived in 1966. He soon became known on the circuit by taking part in lengthy jam sessions at Zoot Money's house. Chandler introduced Hendrix to bass player Noel Redding and drummer Mitch Mitchell, and they began playing together as the Jimi Hendrix Experience. Kit Lambert was so impressed by a set he saw at the Scotch of St James Club that he wanted to sign the band to his new Track label. But since Track was not due to get off the ground for another few months, the first single by the Experience, *Hey Joe*, came out instead on Polydor. It was an instant chart hit.

His appearance at Monterey established Hendrix in the United States as well. His second single was the classic *Purple Haze*, followed shortly afterwards by the LP set, *Are You Experienced?* By the summer, Hendrix had released *Axis Bold as Love* and his live sets saw the band distorting traditional 12-bar blues into unimagined states.

Jimi Hendrix was an undisputed guitar genius and his showmanship was unmatchable, mixing sex appeal with pop-art violence and wired unpredictability. In 1967, on a live guest spot of the Cilla Black TV show in Great Britain, Hendrix halted *Purple Haze* after a few bars, and led the band into a version of Cream's *Sunshine of Your Love*, to the astonished bemusement of poor Cilla.

Hey Joe and *Purple Haze* were just two of the many classic singles to be released that year. At the height of summer, the haunting sound of *A Whiter Shade of Pale* was a huge hit for Procul Harum. The group had been put together to record the Gary Brooker song, and they never equalled its ethereal swirl. The record was played constantly by John Lennon as he was driven around in his multi-coloured Rolls Royce, but it was Lennon's *All You Need Is Love* that was to become the anthem of the flower power generation.

FAR LEFT
The Jimi Hendrix experience.

INSET
Jimi enjoys a personalized cigarette.

RIGHT AND BELOW
Janis Joplin lived a hard life to the full, burning out at an early age.

Its simple sentiment and Zen-like truisms – 'there's nothing you can do that can't be done' – combined with elements of the past in its use of big-band horns and the faded refrain of *She Loves You*. When the band performed the song live on *One World*, the first major live satellite TV link-up, it really did seem as though the world was becoming a smaller place: the 'global village'.

The Rolling Stones, as usual, were not far behind. Their single, *We Love You*, managed to jump head first into the hippie/peace/love runaway train, but still maintained their cynical aloofness, with the sardonic tag-line, 'And we hope you love we too'.

One section of the community that did not reciprocate the Stones' love was Britain's Thames Valley drug squad. At the height of the psychedelic summer, they arrested Jagger and Richards on drugs charges. The arrests took place at Richards' country home, Redlands. Richards had invited some friends down to Sussex for the weekend, including Jagger and Marianne Faithfull, and George Harrison and his wife (George became bored after one day, and left on the Saturday evening). The party spent the next day enjoying the expansive grounds at Redlands, which included a large boating lake, while sampling some acid from the United States.

When Keith Richards answered a knock at the door and found 20 or so uniformed police officers outside, he remained calm. He even invited them all in and, amid widespread giggling, announced their presence to his friends, not sure of how much of what was going on was a hallucination.

BELOW
Hendrix, with his trademark upside-down fender stratocaster.

LEFT
Mick Jagger, Marianne Faithfull and Brian Jones.

RIGHT
Mick and Marianne were present at the highly publicized Redlands drug bust.

In fact it was all too real. The officer in charge produced a search warrant and went on to make a thorough check of the premises. Throughout the whole episode Marianne Faithfull lay on the sofa naked, although partly covered by a fur rug – a high point of the media coverage of the incident.

The case came to court with Jagger charged with possession and Richards with allowing drugs to be consumed on his premises; both were shocked to receive custodial sentences. Richards later boasted of his respectful treatment from fellow inmates, but Jagger found it a harsh and frightening development.

However, there was a general public outcry over the severity of the sentences. The concept of 'fair play', deep rooted in the British psyche, questioned whether the pair would have been treated in the same way had they been unknown. Many felt that they were being held up as an example to others.

William Rees Mogg took the unusual and unprecedented step of writing a strongly-worded leader in the London *Times* on the subject, under the heading 'Who would crush a butterfly on a wheel?' The following week, a full-page advertisement appeared in the paper with the message 'Legalize Cannabis'. It was endorsed with the signature of many famous figures, including all four Beatles. The Who released a single in support, with royalties going towards a fighting fund.

When the cases came up on appeal, both sentences were quashed; Jagger and Richards left the court with barely hidden relief.

The incident was an indication of how quickly opinions were changing, and 1967 was an extremely creative year. Late in 1966 the Beach Boys had released *Good Vibrations*. The song was a global best seller, and took the single format to new dimensions. Brian Wilson had masterminded the piece, which had started out as a straightforward R&B tune, but by the time it reached the public's ears it was a multi-tracked epic, featuring tempo changes, strange swirling electronic passages, dreamy organ-led sequences and, of course, the tightly-arranged soaring harmonies. After the artistic accolades that had fallen on *Pet Sounds*, Brian Wilson had moved the group on to different ground entirely. It was a taste of things to come.

Good Vibrations had taken many hours of studio time to complete, and was culled from the now legendary *Smile* sessions. This album was to be Brian Wilson's masterpiece. His arrangements, together with Van Dyke Parks' orchestrations, took the music beyond rock and pop boundaries into a new area that recognized no exclusive limits.

FAR LEFT
The Beach Boys pictured in the middle of some home improvements.

BELOW
John Lennon's multi-coloured Rolls Royce parked on London's King's Road.

ABOVE AND OPPOSITE
By 1967 it was hip to personalize anything by painting it in psychedelic colours

But Wilson's mind was in a highly confused state. Legend has it that he destroyed the tapes of *Smile* after becoming obsessed with his belief in the magical power of the track *Fire*. Some fragments, like *Heroes and Villains* and the later released *Surf's Up* give glimpses of the work *Smile* might have been, and the effect it might have had can only be guessed at.

The Beatles were left to take the initiative. The album they put out in the summer of 1967 was *Sergeant Pepper's Lonely Hearts Club Band*, and is widely acknowledged as the most important rock album ever made. The idea behind the project came from Paul McCartney. He wanted the record to have a continuous theme running through it, a concept. The album took eight months to record. Unlike the Stones, who had already started recording in superior American studios, the Beatles continued to work at the EMI owned studio in Abbey Road in London. The huge sound rooms had been built to accommodate orchestras and big bands, with the outdated control rooms up flights of stairs. The technology was such that even a simple playback required half-an-hour of rewiring.

But the sessions took place in a highly creative atmosphere. The band knew what they wanted, and had the time to try and achieve it. *Strawberry Fields Forever*, recorded at an earlier session for inclusion on the album, was released as a single, and shows how the group were working. Lennon's song had been recorded in two widely differing formats, both having some of the required effect, but neither capturing the song's intended spirit completely. So the two versions were spliced together to produce the finished version.

The songs that Lennon and McCartney were taking to the *Pepper* sessions were their strongest yet, but their treatments were all-important. The writers pushed producer George Martin to the full to bring their ideas to life – the results are plainly heard in the trippy hurdy-gurdy fairground feel of *For the Benefit of Mr Kite*. The lyrics for that particular tune had been lifted almost verbatim from an old circus poster that Lennon had come across.

The resulting album has a rich versatility. McCartney's mawkish traditionalism is to the fore on tracks like *When I'm 64*, but his contemporary eye for detail hits home on *Lovely Rita, Meter*

Maid. Lennon's *Lucy in the Sky with Diamonds* is a journey through a tripped-out soundscape, although he always maintained it was not drug inspired. On *Good Morning Good Morning* he manages to combine a dreary British inevitability with a frustrated creative urge to break away.

The album's strongest moment comes in its closing track. After a brief reprise from Sergeant Pepper and his band, a ponderous piano opens *A Day in the Life.* Snippets from newspapers, cereal packets and television take the listener up to McCartney's middle section, which slaps back to real life with a sleepy breakfast and a run for the bus. A puff of smoke upstairs drifts back to Lennon's dreamworld, with the line 'I'd love to turn you on'. The end is a euphoric rush, achieved by George Martin's use of the orchestra, giving them a starting point and a place to end, letting each instrument find its own way. The result is an enveloping wave of sound, ending in a slowly decaying piano chord hit by many hands.

It wasn't only the music that set the album apart. The concept extended to the packaging too. The end product was not as impressive as the band wished, due to financial constraints from EMI, but the package still included cut-out-and-keep souvenirs, and the lyrics reproduced for the first time. The idea behind the sleeve was to present a collection of the Beatles' own personal pop icons. Each member supplied a list, except for Ringo – 'Anything the others want is fine by me' – with only a few, such as John's inclusion of Hitler, being vetoed. The final sleeve contains images of Ghandi, Monroe, W C Fields, Brando, Dylan, Lawrence of Arabia, Oscar Wilde, and Stu Sutcliffe.

The sleeve was designed by top pop-artist Peter Blake. The actual art session was not a great success, with the expensive flower arrangements quickly wilting under the studio lights, and with

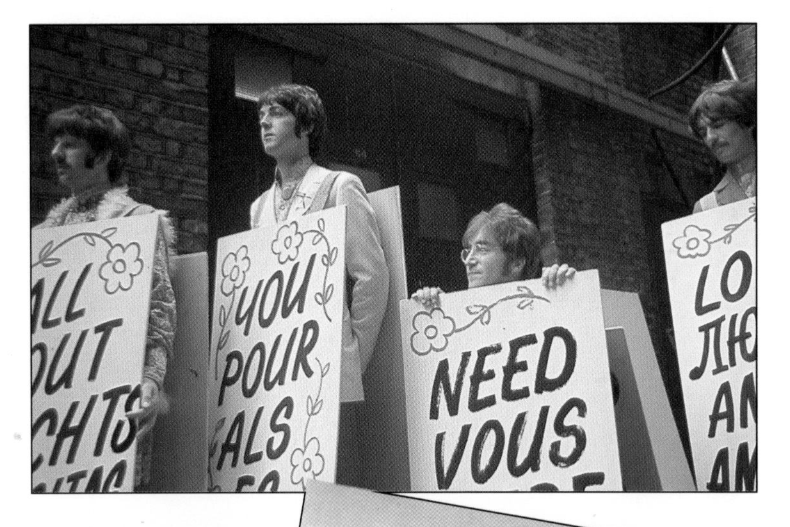

some figures withholding their consent to be included. But the end result was hailed as much as the music that was contained within it.

Sergeant Pepper was an unprecedented artistic and commercial success. In one fell swoop, it again established the Beatles as being far ahead of the field, and set the seal on their transition from hysteria-generating pop-stars to acclaimed, accepted artists. The album became *the* record that encapsulated the sound of 'The Summer of Love'.

ABOVE
The Beatles 'All You Need is Love' was a message with international appeal.

RIGHT
The 'Sgt. Pepper' sleeve was almost as important as the record it contained.

FAR RIGHT
The group were once again established as the leaders of their field.

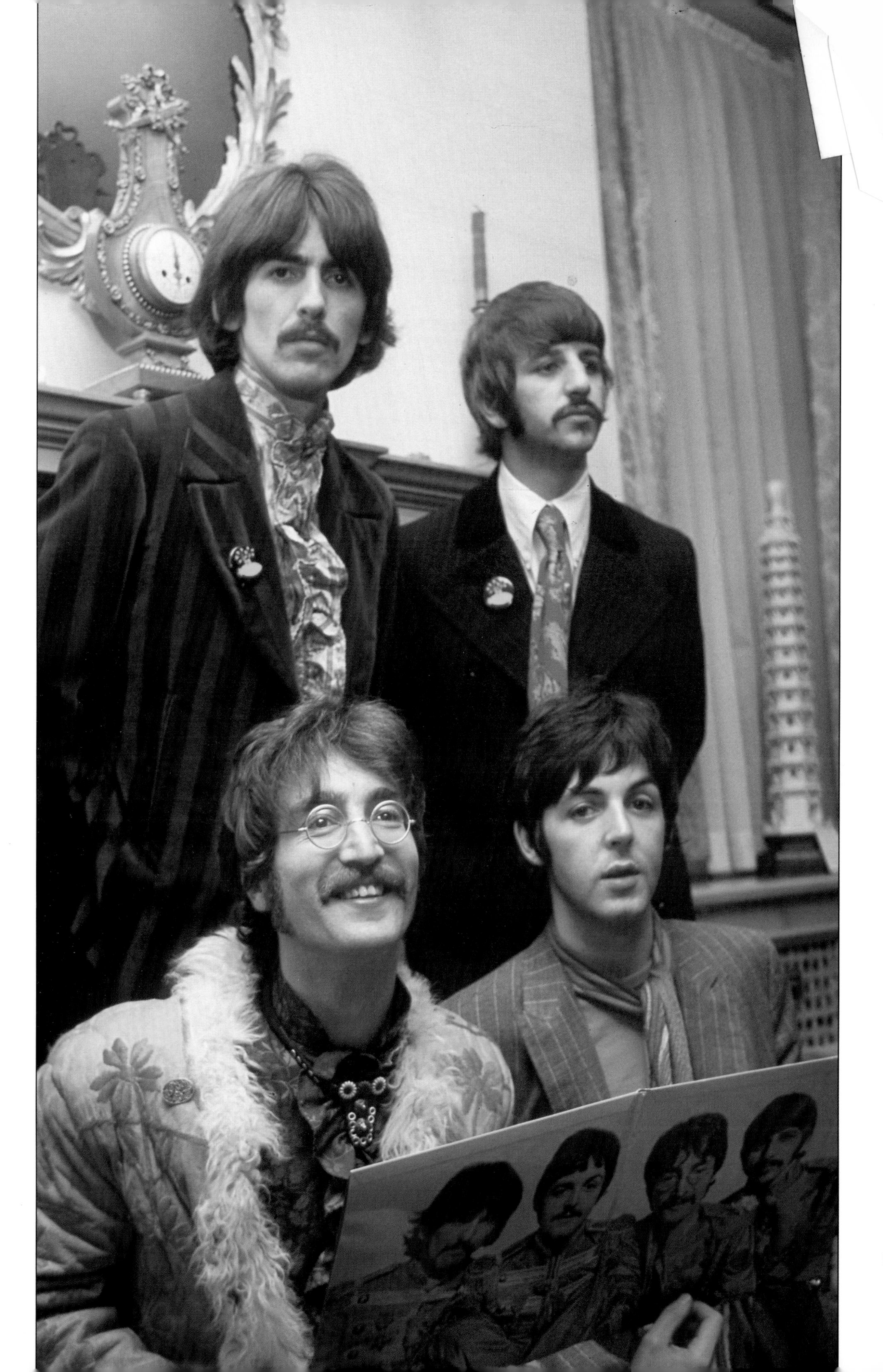

HEROES AND VILLAINS 8

The 1960s saw a considerable number of the hippie movement turning to the East for inspiration, reflected in the craze for joss-sticks, incense and flowing clothes, but more often representing an inner search for fulfilment. George Harrison steered the Beatles in that direction, playing sitar on tracks as early as the *Revolver* album. Harrison's contribution to *Sergeant Pepper* was the highly derivative *Within You Without You*, an Indian-inspired raga recorded as a tribute to his friend Ravi Shankar.

By 1967, the general interest in things Eastern had extended to the teaching and philosophy of its religious wise men. One such was the Himalayan Maharishi Mahesh Yogi. The Beatles first came into contact with the guru when he held introductory sessions at the Hilton Hotel in London to explain his teachings, based on a renunciation of worldly goods and reliance on transcendental meditation.

In a blaze of publicity the Beatles, accompanied by Mick Jagger and his girlfriend Marianne Faithfull, decided to attend a course the Maharishi was holding at Bangor in the Welsh mountains. The world-famous guests arrived by train and took their places in the teacher training college, paying 30s. ($1.50) each for bed and board.

The press went to town, *The Daily Express* reporting an exchange at one of the sessions in typical style. A devotee asked the Maharishi if it is possible to sleep and to know you are asleep the whole night through, to which he replied, 'Yes. It is being asleep and awake together. This is called Cosmic Consciousness.'

But while the group were in Wales, Brian Epstein was found dead in bed at his Belgravia home by his Spanish butler on 27 August, 1967. He was 32-years-old. The Beatles cut short their retreat and returned to London. Paul McCartney appeared upset and shocked, and Lennon commented, 'Our meditation has given us the confidence to withstand such a shock'.

BELOW
The Beatles became enamoured with eastern philosophy – George Harrison and Paul McCartney seen here with the Maharishi.

RIGHT
Brian Epstein's unexpected death made front page news and shocked many.

No. 19,805

EPSTEIN (The Beatle-Making Prince of Pop) DIES AT 32

By TOM TULLETT and DAVID WRIGHT

BRIAN EPSTEIN, the man who made The Beatles, is dead.

The Quiet Prince of Pop, who built up a fantastic multi-million-pound show business empire, was found dead in bed at his £31,000 London home yesterday afternoon.

He was just thirty-two.

And last night Paul McCartney, one of the four Liverpool lads who made Epstein their friend, said:

"This is a great shock. I'm very upset."

Cause of death is still a mystery

Epstein, who always managed to ride the crest of the Liverpool pop wave, was found about 2.45 p.m. by his Spanish butler.

Knock

The butler went to wake him in his second-floor bedroom at the three-storey terrace house in Chapel-street, Belgravia.

He knocked . . . and knocked again. There was no reply. So the butler went inside.

The room was in semi-darkness. The curtains were drawn. And Epstein was in bed.

The butler said later: "Mr Epstein was alone in the house last night. He appeared to be quite well."

Commander John Lawler, head of the No. 1 district, Metropolitan Police, said: "We are treating this as a sudden death.

"There will probably be a post-mortem examination, but this is a matter for the coroner."

And a spokesman for NEMS Enterprises — Epstein's firm that managed The Beatles, Cilla Black, Billy J. Kramer and other big pop names, said:

"The reason for his death is unknown, but there were no untoward circumstances."

Epstein's body left the house in a coffin about 5 p.m. And soon tributes from pop stars and fans began to flow in from all over the world.

Plans

The Beatles—who are in Bangor, North Wales, for the mass rally of a meditation society—made immediate plans to return to London.

Actress Jane Asher, who is with them, held Paul's hand and wept.

Beatle John Lennon said: "Our meditation has given us confidence to withstand such a shock."

George Harrison said: "You cannot pay tribute in words. There is no such thing as death only in the physical sense. Life goes on. The important thing is that he is O.K. now."

[illegible]

The Star Maker—See Centre Pages

THE QUIET MAN FROM LIVERPOOL WHO RAN A 'STABLE' OF STARS

The solace of their new belief was echoed by George Harrison: 'There is no such thing as death, only in the physical sense. Life goes on. The important thing is that he's OK now.'

The truth was that Brian had not been OK for some time. The man the press dubbed 'The Prince of Pop' was deeply unhappy despite his incredible success. He had built up a multi-million pound empire based on a strong stable of artists, but since the Beatles stopped touring he had found himself less involved in the day-to-day running of the group. He felt that he was slowly being left behind. In fact, there was some speculation as to whether the group would sign a new contract with him when the current one ran out that year. His homosexuality, too, had caused him to keep much of his life secret, feeling that unwelcome press may reflect badly on his wholesome protegés, whose attraction to the advice of the Maharishi only served to put them further from his control.

The inquest into his demise returned a verdict of 'accidental death' caused by an overdose of bromide. The drug had been present in a preparation that Epstein had been taking for some time, and had an unforeseen cumulative effect.

When they had recovered from the shock, the Beatles had to decide what to do next, but instead of getting a new manager, the group decided to look after themselves. Paul took on much of the responsibility, using his natural charm on the press and also motivating the other members to look ahead. Their next major project, a follow-up to the most successful album of the decade, was once again McCartney's idea. Originally planned as a feature film, the Magical Mystery Tour was eventually edited for a TV screening on BBC on Boxing Day (December 26) 1967.

The film, a surrealistic drug-fuelled fantasy, was ill-received by press and public alike. The whimsy of *Fool on the Hill* and the pumping wierdness of *I am the Walrus*, combined with fairly gentle pokes at traditional British humour, failed to catch the imagination of the viewers. It was the Beatles' first real flop.

Shaken and directionless, the band once again turned to the Maharishi, visiting the guru at his base in India. But the worldly-wise Ringo returned home only a few days later, saying the centre was like a 'Butlins holiday camp' while the others stayed on, writing many of the songs that surfaced on the *White Album*. They left only after the Maharishi had tried to force his attentions on the actress Mia Farrow.

With the integrity of their guru openly called into question, the Beatles threw themselves into the recording of their next album. By now it was obvious that a big change had occurred within the group. Many of the tracks on the resulting two-record set were more or less solo efforts, with other musicians playing on individual members' songs, sometimes to great effect, as evidenced by Eric Clapton's contribution to Harrison's *While My Guitar Gently Weeps*.

Several thousand miles away, Bob Dylan was emerging from his two years of public silence, although not unproductive time. He had recorded a set of masters with The Band which became known as *The Basement Tapes*. Although not officially released, the set provided hits for others including the songs *Wheels on Fire* and *The Mighty Quinn*. His actual 'comeback' album was the strong *John Wesley Harding*, while The Band released their own album, *Music From The Big Pink*.

LEFT
The Beatles new-found belief in transcendental meditation helped them get over the shock of Epstein's death.

RIGHT
Dylan emerged from his two year hiatus, once again enraging critics and fans alike.

Cream were the first of the 'Supergroups' – Eric Clapton, Jack Bruce and Ginger Baker combined noise with superb technical ability to become one of the world's biggest bands during their short career.

Dylan's next move took the roots' aspect of *John Wesley Harding* a stage further, recording the country-based *Nashville Skyline*.

It was the start of the era of the 'supergroup'. After Eric Clapton had left the Yardbirds to pursue a strictly blues' avenue, he joined John Mayall's Bluesbreakers. But he soon found the format too restricting and, in 1966, he joined jazz-based bass player Jack Bruce and drummer Ginger Baker to form Cream. The London tube system became covered in graffiti proclaiming 'Clapton is God', but the meteoric rise of the band was too much for the volatile mix of characters to stand. By 1968 Clapton had once again moved on, this time to front Blind Faith, with ex-Traffic singer Stevie Winwood.

Meanwhile, the Yardbirds had decided to call it a day. Beck had long since departed, leaving Jimmy Page as the sole guitarist, and by 1968 Keith Relf, Jim Carty and Chris Dreja had had enough. Page was left with the name and a series of live commitments in Scandinavia. Page quickly recruited old session contacts John Paul Jones on bass and John Bonham on drums, and completed the line-up with Birmingham's Robert Plant on vocals. The foursome played the dates as 'The New Yardbirds', but once back in England changed their name to Led Zeppelin, at the suggestion of Keith Moon. The band was based around Page's crushing metal guitar, Bonham's powerhouse rhythms and Plant's expressive mega-blues wail, a formula which quickly gave them success and recognition in the United States.

But the 1968 upheavals covered much more than the music business. All over the world youth rebellion had finally found its voice, and it was out on the streets. There was growing protest against the massive US involvement in the Vietnam war, and in London, hundreds marched on the American Embassy in Grosvenor Square, showing the Metropolitan Police to be pitifully unprepared for such action; in Paris, however, the CRS were in a full state of readiness. When the popular student revolt took to the streets in May the special riot squads dealt with the unrest with violent proficiency; and in Eastern Europe, Russian tanks rolled on to the streets of Prague to halt the reforming Czech government.

On the other side of the Atlantic, the Democratic Convention in Chicago saw running battles in the streets, the arrests of leaders of the hippie movement, and a resulting swing towards Republican

sentiments. At Kent State University the nation was shocked when the National Guard opened fire on students demonstrating against the draft, killing six and wounding many others.

It was all a far cry from the peace and love ideals of only a year earlier, but the hippie-inspired psychedelic scene was not yet over. In London, clubs like the UFO and Gandalf's Garden mixed acid sounds with light-shows and oil-wheel projections, and the group that came to represent this underground scene was Pink Floyd.

Syd Barret, another of the British art school rock-star production line, was attending Beckenham College of art when he, Nick Mason, Roger Waters and Rick Wright formed the Pink Floyd Sound, allegedly named after two Atlanta bluesmen, Pink Council and Floyd Anderson. After shortening the name to

ABOVE AND RIGHT

Led Zeppelin were put together by Jimmy Page from the ashes of the Yardbirds. They enjoyed massive success in the late 1960s, and went on to become the biggest band of the early 1970s.

Pink Floyd, the band became regulars on the London club circuit. They signed to EMI subsidiary Harvest in 1967 and released the classic single *Arnold Layne,* with *See Emily Play* following its predecessor into the Top 30 after its June release.

By the time the group put out their first album, *Piper At The Gates Of Dawn*, they were already being acclaimed as darlings of the avant-garde. But Barrett was suffering from a bad case of drug-induced paranoia and left the band in 1968. His replacement was David Gilmour, and the band's second album, *A Saucerful of Secrets*, although equally successful, pointed to the technical path that awaited the band.

But the one event that truly encapsulated the era of the New Age was

LEFT

Pink Floyd, seen here in their original line-up featuring Syd Barrett, were the ultimate synthesis of British art-school rock and drug-filled psychedelic whimsey. After Barrett's withdrawal from the music scene, the band became one of the pioneers of album based progressive rock that was to dominate much of the 1970s. Barrett remains an enigmatic and revered cult figure.

ABOVE
Riot scenes were a familiar news item in 1968–69.

FAR RIGHT
Woodstock, the new age came of age, with nearly half a million people attending the three day event.

the festival held at Woodstock. From Friday 15 August to Sunday 17 August, 1969, the largest-ever rock festival was held on Max Yasgur's dairy farm in Sullivan County, New York State. Advertised as 'three days of peace and music', the event caught a pulse; more than 200,000 people bought advance tickets. Although the event was very well organized, the actual attendance of 450,000 was way beyond any predictions. It was like a medium-sized city growing up overnight.

When the security fence was breached early on Friday, the organizers had no choice but to declare the event a free festival. The hesitant speech by the man unlucky enough to have to inform the crowd, many of whom had paid, makes for one of the most entertaining moments in the feature film of the event. Nonetheless, the remarkable three days were without any major disturbance, the atmosphere one of cooperation and mutual enjoyment. Most of the major acts associated with the New Age took part, and for many, its enduring image is the version of *The Star Spangled Banner* that Hendrix wrenched from his guitar, the alternative national anthem for the American counter-culture. The event proved it was capable of organizing itself on a massive, although thoroughly alternative, scale.

IT'S ALL OVER NOW, BABY BLUE 9

As the 1960s drew to a close and rock entered a new decade, more names joined that of Brian Epstein on the rock 'n' roll casualty list. Janis Joplin burnt herself out with her demanding lifestyle and Hendrix was soon to follow before disproving those who said he had burnt off his creativity in his few short years at the top. But it was the death of Rolling Stone Brian Jones that seemed to sum up the depressing feel of decay at the time.

Jones was only 25-years-old when he was found dead at the bottom of the swimming pool at his Sussex farmhouse. He had been a strong swimmer and was only separated from his party guests for a matter of minutes. Days before, he had parted company with the Rolling Stones.

For some time, Brian had been at odds with Jagger and Richards over the direction the band should take, and the extent of his involvement in it. In the early days, the Stones had been very much Jones's group. He had been the undisputed leader and the motivating force, seeing a clear mission to take the R&B gospel to the masses.

Jagger had always been suspicious of Jones's musical ability and his enigmatic,

FAR RIGHT
Brian Jones, arguably the most talented Stone.

BELOW
The Rolling Stones on stage in Hyde Park, a few days after the death of Brian Jones.

slightly threatening sexual presence. By the mid-1960s Jagger and Richards were writing most of the Stones' material, and Jones's role was to come up with new influences from different musical cultures, constantly mastering new instruments.

Jones's hedonistic rock star life included his relationship with Anita Pallenberg and his gluttonous drug intake; salacious press stories set him out as the Stone living closest to the edge, but by 1968 Jones was being quietly sidelined in the Stones' camp. He was beginning to be seen by the others as a liability, and Jagger and Richards effectively stage-managed a

ABOVE
Jagger encourages new boy Mick Taylor on stage at Hyde Park.

bloodless coup, establishing themselves as joint leaders of the self-styled 'Greatest Rock and Roll Band in the World'.

Brian Jones's pride could only take so much. When he started turning up for sessions only to find there was no part for him to play, things finally came to a head and the result was that he left the band a few days before his death. Whether or not he would have moved on to become a significant musical force in his own right is open to question, but his influence on the music of the early 1960s cannot be doubted.

The Rolling Stones played their first date without their founder only three days after his death, a huge open air show in London's Hyde Park. In the natural amphitheatre at the southern end of the park the Stones played to over a quarter of a million people, but before the first note was struck, Jagger read a poem by Shelley as a eulogy to Brian Jones. Thousands of butterflies were released from the stage over the heads of the crowd.

Jones's replacement Mick Taylor was understandably nervous and the band was sloppy and under-rehearsed; a picture of thousands of dead butterflies in the cages they had been held in seemed to sum up the dismal event.

Things were running no smoother in the Beatles' camp. Since the death of Epstein

the band seemed to veer from one hitch to the next. The disaster of the *Magical Mystery Tour* had been followed by some solid singles in the form of *Hello Goodbye* and *Lady Madonna*, and the announcement that their future releases would come through their own label, Apple.

The first record on the label was *Hey Jude*. The long, mantra-like refrain once again proved the Beatles as a creative force and the company went on to further success with artists like Mary Hopkin and Badfinger, both of whom McCartney wrote hits for. There was even an Apple shop, selling designer clothes and other merchandise.

ABOVE AND RIGHT
The Beatles now had their own record label, Apple, but splits became highly visible, with each member taking on an increasing profile outside the group.

The Beatles, released in 1969 and which became known as *The White Album*, pointed to changes taking place in the band, both musically and individually. Paul made an unpopular move when he married New York photographer Linda Eastman, and George and his wife Patti were arrested for drug possession the day after the wedding. John had already left his wife Cynthia and started living with avant-garde Japanese artist Yoko Ono, who consumed much of his time and diverted his attentions away from the group.

The confused state of the band's financial affairs forced them to seek help. McCartney was keen to involve Linda's family in the business, but the other Beatles had been greatly impressed with the talents of American trouble-shooter Alan Klein. Klein already managed the Stones and had a hard reputation for winning his clients good, renegotiated deals. Jagger had recommended him to Lennon, and Klein's forthright manner struck an immediate chord with him.

Although McCartney had reservations, it was eventually agreed that Klein should look into the band's affairs, with limited access also for the Eastmans. In his first year, Klein earned the Beatles more money than they had received in all their previous years put together. Few of Epstein's earlier deals had been advantageous to the group, and many people had grown rich on the Beatles' backs. Klein also pointed out that the whole Apple set-up was an expensive white elephant, with the result that the scale of the operation was toned down, the shop closed and many of the original altruistic ideas shelved.

BELOW AND FAR RIGHT
Lennon began to court publicity outside the Beatles, with his Dada-esque 'bed-ins' and 'bag-ins' with conceptual artist wife Yoko Ono drawing the attention of the world's media.

HAIR PEACE.
BED PEACE.

JOHN LENNON MBE BACK TO T

Once again motivated by McCartney, the group gathered in Pinewood studios to begin rehearsals for a new album. The set was to follow along the lines of the aborted *Get Back* collection, which had gone as far as a finished track listing and sleeve, featuring the band in a reshoot of the *Please Please Me* cover at EMI headquarters in Manchester Square.

Let It Be was to be a return to basics for the band. The idea was to record with no other musicians and few overdubs, although black American keyboard player Billy Preston was brought in towards the end of the sessions. From the start, the project was fraught with tension. The soundstage at Pinewood was cold and inhibiting, and the ever-present film cameras intended to document proceedings for a TV special were intrusive. Lennon in particular seemed to lack motivation, with the constant presence of Yoko causing arguments and resentment from the others. Lennon lacked new songs, reworking *One After 909* an early 1950s original instead, and *Across the Universe*, first recorded for a charity project in 1967.

The sessions were eventually abandoned, although the tapes were later given to Phil Spector who sifted hundreds of hours to produce the last official Beatles release of new material, *Let It Be*. But the band had one more stab at recording, and the resulting *Abbey Road* is considered by many fans as their finest work. The richness of the material catches the Beatles at their most productive. From the opening grind of *Come Together* to the sublime beauty of *Something*, which was the only 'A' side written by George Harrison, the whole album glides along on a warm, assured professionalism. On side 2, fragments of tunes are woven into a seamless medley, ending with McCartney's words:

'Then in the end
The love you take
Is equal to the love you make.'

By the time the record was released, the four Beatles were well set on their individual paths. Harrison had been the first to release a solo album, the experimental *Electronic Sounds* on Apple subsidiary Zapple. He followed it with a collection of mainly Indian-inspired tracks on the soundtrack to the film *Wonderwall*. John Lennon embarked on his world peace mission with Yoko, gaining constant press coverage with their hotel 'bed-ins' and 'bag-ins'. On one such trip to Toronto, he recorded *Give Peace a Chance* under the banner of the Plastic Ono Band.

The band went on to release *Cold Turkey* in October 1969, recorded with a loose grouping which included Eric Clapton, old friend Klaus Voorman on bass, and Alan White on drums. Clapton's raw, screaming guitar and Lennon's agonized vocal take the listener through an aural version of drug withdrawal.

That November, Lennon returned his MBE to Buckingham Palace with a note explaining the gesture was a protest against Great Britain's failure to condemn America's continued involvement in Vietnam, and to show his displeasure at *Cold Turkey* slipping down the charts. The great British public thought Lennon was quite mad.

1970 saw the release of *Let It Be*, but the Beatles themselves seemed to take little interest in either film or record, with none

NDS HIS E QUEEN

By JAMES WILSON

BEATLE John Lennon sent his M B E medal back to the Queen yesterday—wrapped in an envelope and delivered to Buckingham Palace in his white Mercedes.

With it was a letter to the Queen explaining why he was returning the award, which he received with the other Beatles in 1965.

The letter said: "I am returning this MBE in protest against Britain's involvement in the Nigeria-Biafra thing, against our support of America in Vietnam . . . and against 'Cold Turkey' slipping down the charts."

"Cold Turkey" is the latest record by John and his wife Yoko Ono. It is now in the charts at number 16.

Copies of the letter—signed "with love, John Lennon"—have been sent to Prime Minister Harold Wilson and the Central Chancery, which is responsible for listing honours awards.

Last night John—his wife by his side—said: "I feel very strongly about peace. This gesture is really a publicity gimmick for peace.

Squirmed

"I did not really want to take the award in the first place, but something in my ego told me I might be able to use it one day—and now I have.

"I always squirmed when I saw 'MBE' on my letters. I did not really belong to that sort of world. It always embarrassed me.

"I think the Establishment bought the Beatles with it. Now I am giving it back, thank you very much."

John, 28, said the decision to return the award came in bed early yesterday. "I was turning over thoughts of the wars and the report of the atrocities in Vietnam. I have just returned from holiday and was feeling guilty about doing that instead of working for peace.

"I have been thinking about returning it for some time. Suddenly, I thought 'now's the time.'"

He continued: "I am sure my fans will realise that this decision is my business."

Why did he return the M B E in an envelope? John said: "I have been wearing it on my belt along with other hippie things. I lost the box and had to return it in the envelope."

Thirty-four-year-old Yoko said: "I am very proud. This is what I like about John. He is just being very natural. Both of us have the same vibration about this."

A spokesman for Apple, the Beatles' company, said the reference to "Cold Turkey" in the letter was included as an "afterthought."

Items

"John saw that the disc had slipped a place down the charts and decided to add this to his protest. There is no intention that the other two items and this should have the same significance."

A Buckingham Palace spokesman said last night: "People are entitled to return awards. In fact several people did so when it was announced that the Beatles had been awarded M B Es."

of them attending the latter's West End première. Just after the release of the Beatles' album, McCartney put out his own self-titled LP, with Paul playing all the instruments. That year also saw Ringo release two albums, the collection of standards, *Sentimental Journey*, and the follow-up *Beaucoup De Blues*. Harrison set a precedent by releasing a three-album boxed set, containing many songs he had not been able to put to use in the Beatles. *All Things Must Pass* was very widely acclaimed, and featured contributions from Klaus Voorman, Eric Clapton and Ringo, among many others.

Lennon was not to be outdone. His release that year was *John Lennon/ Plastic Ono Band*, more usually referred to as the *Mother* album. It was a set of stripped-down, intensely personal songs whose primary influence was that of the Janov therapy, whereby patients were encouraged to regress to hidden childhood fears, and release them in a terrifying 'primal scream'. The LP includes classics like *Working Class Hero* and *God*, in which Lennon declares that all he believes in is 'me, Yoko and me'.

By this time, the normal functions of the Beatles had broken down, and the members were only talking through their lawyers. Late in the year, the inevitable happened: Paul McCartney took the matter to court, dissolved the partnership, and called in the official receiver. Accused of being the one to break up the Beatles, McCartney declared, 'I didn't leave the Beatles, the Beatles left the Beatles, but nobody wants to say the party's over. The acrimonious end of the group had no silver lining, as it seemed that the 1960s were winding up and breaking down in every direction.

In Las Vegas, a parody of the King was performing to the supper-club circuit. Elvis had never managed to recapture his former glory after his discharge from the army in 1963 (indeed Lennon later said that Elvis had died the day he was conscripted in 1960), and throughout the second half of the decade, Presley slipped further away from his original dynamism.

A steady stream of exploitive Hollywood films and the relative stranglehold that

Images of the King from the Hollywood years – many fans blamed Colonel Parker for emasculating Presley by forcing him into unsuitable film roles.

Colonel Tom Parker held over his charge ensured a stream of second-rate record releases. By the mid-1960s things were so bad that RCA were releasing material recorded in the 1950s but rejected as sub-standard at the time. A few valiant tries at resuscitating the King's credibility included his first TV special since his appearance with Frank Sinatra. Elvis appeared coast-to-coast with *Aloha from Hawaii*, *Burning Love*, *Suspicious Minds* and *In the Ghetto*, good singles that went some way to showing there were still embers of the old fire. But the easy money of the Las Vegas circuit made Elvis content to play up to the fantasies of the blue-rinse matrons. Dressed in outrageous superhero costumes, he lived in a pretend world, where meeting the US President and gaining honorary membership of the FBI were more interesting than rebuilding his career.

With the Beatles disintegrating and Elvis a rock 'n' roll zombie, the heavyweight title was open for the Stones to take once and for all. But they too were floundering following Jones's death, with tales of drug abuse and rockstar excess reaching new levels of the absurd.

In December 1969, they agreed to interrupt a highly-grossing tour of the United States to perform a one-off free show in San Francisco. The gesture was an attempt to show some link with the anti-materialistic counter-culture, and was to be co-headlined with the Grateful Dead, but the venue was changed at very short notice. The eventual site chosen was the Altamont speedway track in Alamenda County, California.

There were problems from the outset, with the provision of proper facilities impossible at such short notice. Most ominous of all, the Stones' tour manager, Sam Cutler, decided to engage the local Hell's Angels to police the event for a payment of $500 worth of beer. During the opening set by Santana, there were ugly scenes in the crowd. The stage was low enough to be easily accessible and a constant stream of Angels moved from the stage to the audience and back again. By the time Jefferson Airplane took the stage there was an air of violence and conflict. The 'security' seemed to be giving out motiveless beatings, and when Airplane singer Marty Balin remonstrated with the Angels one of them took to the stage and beat him unconscious with a pool cue. The other members of the band played on, but by now it was quite clear who was in control of the event.

The Grateful Dead performed without major incident, but there was a long gap before the appearance of the Stones. Some felt that they were trying to let the situation cool down, Jagger having already been punched in the mouth, but others felt that they were waiting for darkness to heighten the arrival of their 'Satanic Majesties'

The air was electric by the time the band finally took to the stage. Jagger looked nervous and barely in control as he stood surrounded by the Angels, many of whom openly jeered his performance.

When the band launched into *Sympathy for the Devil* it was clear there was a major disturbance only yards from the stage. Cameras rolling for the resultant film, *Gimme Shelter*, captured the full horror as a young black man, Meredith Hunter, can clearly be seen running through the crowd. Chased by a Hell's Angel who stabs

FAR LEFT
Elvis attempted a credible come-back, which although a commercial failure in his terms, produced fine singles such as 'Burning Love'.

ABOVE AND LEFT
In later years Presley became an embarrassing parody of his former self.

him in the back, Hunter turns on his attacker directly in front of the stage and pulls a gun; almost instantly he is surrounded by a mob of Angels and is repeatedly stabbed until he dies.

Jagger did not see the incident, but the whole crowd soon became aware that something very serious had taken place. A deep shadow was cast over the whole ethos of the New Age; whereas Woodstock had been a glimpse of the Aquarian ideal and had shown the counter-culture could organize itself, Altamont showed the reverse, to symbolize the end of the 1960s Age of Innocence. It was a brutal re-awakening into the violence of the real world.

Elsewhere, Pink Floyd were leading the way into the realms of 'progressive rock' with the release of *Ummagumma*. With two sides recorded live and the remainder given over to indulgent stereo trickery, the album was a distinct pointer to the way 'the album' would develop through the 1970s, culminating with Pink Floyd's all-time best seller, *Dark Side of the Moon*.

The Who had already taken the idea of the concept album one stage further with the release of *Tommy*. Frustrated with the limitations of the three-minute pop single, Townshend had undertaken to write a 'rock opera'. Although the success of the project proved him right, it represented a turnaround from his position on over-production and quest for simplicity.

Led Zeppelin were establishing themselves as one of the world's truly great live attractions. Their first few albums relied heavily on Bonham's pounding patterns and Page's electric mixtures of styles, and the band were at the forefront of the expanding and exploding heavy rock metal market.

But the emergence of these progressive, album-based groups resulted in the decline of the 45 rpm single. By the end of the 1960s, single sales were steadily decreasing, and with them the very heart

ABOVE
The Stones on stage at the ill-fated Altamont show.

RIGHT
One of the many ugly scenes from Altamont.

FAR RIGHT
One small step from Neil Armstrong gave the world an outsider's view of the global village, and signified the end of the 1960s.

of 'pop' seemed to be fading. Groups such as Pink Floyd and Led Zeppelin failed to release any tracks in the single format over the following years. The music industry had realized that the big money was to be found in the album market, and singles began to be treated more and more as poor relations, promotional adverts instead of three-minute innovative air time that it was earlier in the decade.

The 1960s were dead, and times really were changing. Neil Armstrong had taken his one small step on the moon, making the world seem even smaller than ever, when the start of the 1970s saw a new wave of groups taking hold of the reins. A new generation of consumers with drastically different tastes and demands to those of their older brothers and sisters ensured that the first Golden Age of Rock was well and truly over.

INDEX

Italic numerals refer to illustrations or their captions

B

C

E

ACKNOWLEDGEMENTS

The author and publishers would like to thank the following for granting permission to use photographs in this book.
Marvin Gaye/Berry Gordy Jnr Enterprises Inc *p 80 above;*
Old Gold Archives, *pp 6 right and below, 11, 33, 34, 35 below left, 37 above right, 38, 39, 56, 58 below;*
Metro Music *p 84 below right;*
Movie Star News, 134 West 18th Street, New York *pp 6 above right, 16, 111;*
Pictorial Press *pp 6 above left, middle left, 7, 9 above and below, 10, 12 above, below left, below right, 13, 16–17 below, 17 above, 19, 20, 21 above and below, 22, 23, 24, 25, 26, 27, 28, 30 above and below, 32, 36 above left, below, 37 left, 43, 44, 45, 46, 47, 48, 49, 50 above and below, 51 below, 52 all pictures, 53 below, 54 all pictures, 55 above left, above right, below, 57, 58 above, 59 above and below, 60, 61 above and below, 64–5 all pictures, 66 above and below, 67, 68–9, 71, 72 left, 73, 74 below left, 80 below, 81, 82, 83, 85, 86, 87 above left, above right, below, 88 above and below, 90 main picture, 91 below, 92, 93 above and below, 94, 95, 96, 97, 98 above, 99, 100, 102, 103, 104 left, 104–5, 106, 106–7, 108–9, 112–13, 113 right, 114, 115 above and below, 116, 117, 120 all pictures, 121 all pictures, 122, 123 above and below, 125 below;*